AF471462

EXPLORING MICHIGAN'S UPPER PENINSULA COASTS

ST. MARYS RIVER, LAKE SUPERIOR, AND NORTHERN LAKE MICHIGAN COASTS

INCLUDES ST. IGNACE, SAULT STE. MARIE, MARQUETTE, ESCANABA, AND OTHER COASTAL U.P. CITIES

LENKK PRESS

Cover Design: Bob Royce
Cover Photo of Spray Falls courtesy of Tim Trombley,
www.greatlakesphotography.net
Editor: Violet Moore
ISBN 979-8-9855037-1-5

For Bob

I don’t deserve such a terrific husband. You could do better but don’t even think about it.

You made traveling the Upper Peninsula a romantic adventure.

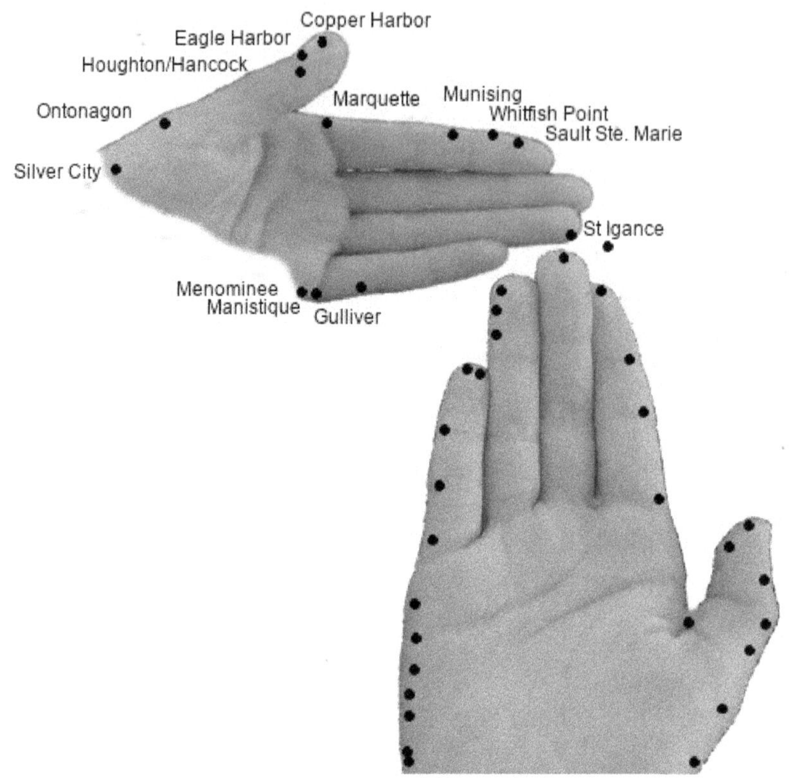

Michigan Hand Map
with Upper Peninsula Cities

Four Largest Cities in Michigan's Upper Peninsula
from worldpopulationreview.com 2019 census lists.

Marquette 20,866

Sault St. Marie 13,445

Escanaba 12,160

Menominee 8,599

Table of Contents

Book Two
Exploring Michigan's
Upper Peninsula Coasts

(Lake Huron background is included in Book One of this travel series.)

Introduction and Overview

Julie Royce wrote and compiled two travel books in the early 2000s. The first was devoted to Michigan's Thumb where she was born and raised. The second covered Lake Michigan's Sunset Coast. She intended to make the Upper Peninsula the subject of a third book, but her plans were delayed by a job-related move to California.

When she finally returned her attention to her home state, the world had changed. Today's travelers have phone apps and the internet for lodging, restaurant, and shopping information.

The upside of the tech world is immediacy. By the time Royce's earlier books were published, several places had closed or been replaced by new businesses. Only the background and local stories remained interesting.

Thus was born the idea of a traveler's companion to Michigan's Great Lakes coasts. It would encompass a journey starting on I-75 in Michigan's southeast corner, traveling along Lake Erie, the Detroit River, Lake St. Clair, the St. Clair River, Lake Huron, the St. Marys River, Lake Superior, and Lake Michigan to Michigan's southwest point.

Exploring Michigan's Upper Peninsula Coasts includes city histories, museums, parks, beaches, lighthouses, ghost stories, shipwrecks, stories about the famous or infamous with ties to the area, and movies and books set in the Michigan locale you are visiting. For example, *Anatomy of a Murder* was filmed in Big Bay, Marquette, Ishpeming, and Michigamme in the Upper Peninsula.

It is the author's hope that this volume sprinkles flavor on the cities and places visited, and that your adventures along Michigan's waterways add many unique experiences to your travel repertoire.

Royce did not add a bibliography. Much of what is included in this guide is stories—no way to prove or disprove the truth. While she has tried to research carefully, this is not meant to be a reference book.

Legends. The following categories have been included, as applicable, for each city or stop:

- MUSEUMS
- BEACHES, PARKS, AND TRAILS
- OTHER STOPS TO CONSIDER
- LIGHTHOUSES
- SHIPWRECKS
- THE FAMOUS OR INFAMOUS WITH TIES TO THE CITY
- BOOKS AND MOVIES WITH TIES TO THE CITY
- GHOST STORIES

Welcome to Michigan. Courtesy of Bob Royce.

1. The Mighty Mac

If you have been traveling the coastlines of Michigan's Great Lakes Waterway system by automobile, you will now cross from Michigan's Lower Peninsula to the Upper Peninsula.

In Mackinaw City, you have savored many fabulous views of the Mackinac Bridge, a notable site in its own right. Now you get to experience driving across the five-mile expanse.

The Mackinac Bridge. Courtesy of Gary Martin.

Opened to traffic on November 1, 1957, the 26,372-foot-long bridge, the longest suspension bridge between anchorages in the Western Hemisphere, spans the Straits of Mackinac connecting Mackinaw City with St. Ignace. Prior to the bridge construction, ferries were the main means of connection between peninsulas. In the early 1900s, with the advent of more highways and a greater desire to travel, a need grew for a simpler, faster way to cross the straits.

The State of Michigan first initiated an automobile ferry service between Mackinaw City and St. Ignace in 1923. At its peak the ferry system operated nine boats that carried as many as 9,000 vehicles a day. Traffic backups could stretch as long as 16 miles.

As early as the 1800s, Michiganders dreamed of a bridge. Engineers studied the possibilities in the 1930s, debating whether it should or could be constructed. Funding issues delayed the project. Finally, the engineering marvel began to take shape. Construction started in 1954, and three years later the bridge was a reality.

Five men died during construction of the bridge, one from the bends when he surfaced too quickly from the bottom where he was placing pilings. The other four were killed when they fell. A plaque memorializes their deaths. Two autos have gone over the sides of the bridge, the cause of one determined to be losing control while driving too fast, and the other a suicide. Suicide, however, is rare on the bridge, maybe a dozen in total have jumped. One small plane crashed into the bridge's suspension cables. All three aboard died.

Building the Mighty Mac was a feature-length documentary produced by Hollywood filmmaker Mark Howell in 1997. PBS aired the film. The History Channel also produced a feature (2003) on *Modern Marvels* and included a segment on the bridge.

The Mackinac Bridge Authority driver assistance program provides drivers for those with gephyrophobia—a fear of driving across a bridge. The service can be used by anyone more comfortable having someone chauffeur them from one shore to the other. More than a thousand people use this service each year. The program was discontinued indefinitely during the coronavirus pandemic. If you desire assistance, check its current availability.

On Labor Day, the bridge is opened to walkers. Traditionally, the governor leads thousands of people on the five-mile walk from Mackinaw City to St. Ignace.

The U.P.

As you cross into the Upper Peninsula, consider a few tips to make your travel more fun. First of all, if you are a Type A personality, you may find that time seems to move slower in parts of the U.P. But isn't that what you want on vacation?

In the out-of-the-way dots on the map, things are not the same as they are in the big city. Again, you are taking a break from your hectic routine so smile and enjoy. Booking a motel is a good example.

You may not receive an email confirmation but just a reference number that you need to write down. If you are sent a confirmation email, there may be no address for the motel on it, so, again, make notes during the telephone booking. You may be told that if you plan to arrive after 6:00 p.m., they'll leave the door to your room unlocked and a key inside. As you drive toward your destination, you may smile at road signs that warn, "Snowmobiles 30 mph."

A word about **Dark Skies**. A dark sky is the perfect place to stargaze. It is a land area where the air above has not been polluted by man-made illumination. When the sun sets, and the moon starts its shift, one of Michigan's six dark sky parks will provide you with the most amazing star shows in the country. The dark sky parks are protected dark sky areas, but most of the Upper Peninsula is shrouded in near complete darkness during nighttime hours. You will see the Milky Way and the Aurora Borealis like never before.

Welcome to Michigan's U.P.

How the U.P. Became Part of Michigan

Once upon a time, while Michigan's statehood was pending, and Ohio was already a state, the two feuded over who owned the Toledo Strip.

The U.P. at that time? Not so important and not on anyone's mind. The Toledo Strip, however, was a port, and the land that surrounded it connected the Great Lakes to the Ohio-Mississippi trade network. That was worth fighting over.

Ohio and Michigan aimed threats at each other. They called up their respective militias to settle the squabble. A few random shots were fired. The brouhaha was named the Toledo War of 1835-36. President Andrew Jackson, hoping to avoid bloodshed, intervened and knowing which side of the election bread was buttered, he supported Ohio.

Feeling he had to toss Michigan a bone to ease the loss, he proposed that Ohio stop obstructing Michigan's petition for statehood, and he threw in the Upper Peninsula as a bonus.

As it turned out, Michigan made a pretty good deal after all.

Da Yoop (U.P.) and Yoopers

Yooper refers to a native or resident of the Upper Peninsula of Michigan. You'll love the spice and color Yooper lingo adds to conversation, yah?

Ending declaratory sentences with yah or eh, thus turning them into questions is a decidedly Yooper twist. Living in a climate often described as eight months of winter, Yoopers don't just withstand the cold, they embrace it—snowmobiling, sledding, dog sled races, outhouse races, cross-country skiing. If it requires ice and snow, they're in, you betcha.

Yooper English differs from standard English because of the linguistic background of Finnish and other Scandinavian settlers to the area. Almost half the Finnish immigrants to the U.S. settled in the Upper Peninsula. Some Yoopers insist Finglish is the official language of Da Yoop.

One resourceful Yooper spent nearly a decade arguing the word Yooper should be added to the Merriam-Webster Dictionary. Motivating his crusade was a desire to use the word in Scrabble© games. He succeeded when Yooper was one of 150 new words added to the 11th Edition of *Merriam-Webster's Collegiate Dictionary*. The problem is that Yooper is a proper noun and the *Official Scrabble Player's Dictionary* might not allow its use, but let's not rain on this dedicated man's parade.

Do not make the mistake of thinking trolls (Michiganders from below the bridge) consider their Yooper brethren brainless hicks who love nothing but drinking beer and hunting. Those pastimes are fine, but Da Yoop is full of interesting residents. Marquette, a university town on Lake Superior, is well known for art galleries, shopping, theater, microbreweries, and even restaurants with vegan menus. Yoopers have a sense of humor and try not to take life too seriously. They appreciate the beauty of their peninsula, and many enjoy the slower pace of life along with enough room to stretch their arms without hitting their neighbor's shoulder. Even if they smile and accuse you of being from overseas, they'll welcome you like a long-lost friend.

As you prepare to enter Da Yoop, you can go online and find a Yooper Dictionary or buy one at any of the bookstores in Da Yoop. To get you thinking like a Yooper, here are some helpful hints to keep in mind:

Replace "th" with "d" (*dere* for *there*, *dat* for *that*, *dos* for *those*, and *dem* for them). De udders are not a part of a cow's anatomy.

Remember, da Bears are da football team da Yoopers hate da most, and da Pack are da football team da Yoopers love da most.

A few words you can throw into your conversation to impress your new Yooper friends:

Kromer, kind of cap with ear flaps and lined with felt.

Overseas is anything sout' of da bridge.

Pasty or Pasties are a major form of sustenance for Yoopers although popular throughout the state. If you order one of these delicious half-moon-shaped pies, pronunciation is critical. Make sure you ask for a *pass tee* not a *pā-stē*. *Pass tees* are not a circle-shaped item of clothing the size of a quarter with the designated purpose of maintaining a stripper's dignity. The Yooper pasty or pastie is of Cornish origin and consists of meat filling with potatoes and rutabagas or carrots stuffed inside a flaky crust. (See the recipes in the appendix to try your hand at making a pasty.) The savory turnovers spiced with salt and pepper were carried by miners in their lunch pails for hearty noon meals. They are so revered that every Michigander is required to eat one before dying. It's part of the Michigan Compiled Laws. But don't try to look it up.

Pre'ner. A contraction meaning pretty near. We're pre'ner there.

Tinking. What you do when you put your brain in gear.

Ya know means don't you agree?

Youse means more than one person.

If you still are having trouble imagining the conversations, think Francis McDormand in *Fargo*. True, that was North Dakota, but the idioms seem pure Yooper.

2. St. Ignace

Saint Ignace (usually written St. Ignace), 2020 population 2,452, sits on the Lake Huron northern shoreline, the first city you enter in the Upper Peninsula. It is one of two ports with ferry service to Mackinac Island, and the only mainland city accessible from Mackinac Island by snowmobile when Lake Huron freezes over. Ferry service is often not an option from late October through early May.

Winter temperatures with windchill factored in frequently fall below zero. The permanent residents of Mackinac Island depend on an ice bridge to make it to the mainland. Usually about February, someone heads out to test the solidity of the ice. If they make it half way to St. Ignace, they call back to report the good news before continuing their trek. Islanders drag discarded Christmas trees onto the ice to mark the bridge path.

Ojibwe (also Ojibwa) and Odawa headquarters are in St. Ignace where Native Americans comprise one-third of the local population. Father Jacques Marquette, a Jesuit priest, established a mission in St. Ignace about 1671. The priest is buried at the site. The mission is now the Museum of Ojibwa Culture.

The Ojibwe dominated the fur trade in the seventeenth century and allied themselves with the French in the Seven Years War against the British. The French were defeated, losing control of the fur trade to the British who then maintained power until the Americans ousted the Brits in the Revolutionary War. The area became part of the Northwest Territory of the new United States.

The late 1800s brought the end of the fur trade and ushered in a new tourist-based economy boosted by proximity and ferry service to popular Mackinac Island. Lodging is less expensive in St. Ignace than on the Island so many people book accommodations in St. Ignace and ferry to the Island. (See Mackinac Island in Book One).

The Kewadin Casino is a significant tourist attraction and a big local employer.

• Museums

Fort De Baude Museum, 334 North State Street, showcases more than 3,500 artifacts including weapons, trade items, arrowheads, and beadworks. Visit 8,000 years of history in fascinating dioramas. Learn how the region and times impacted the Native Anishinaabe people.

<<>>

The Museum of Ojibwa Culture (spelled Ojibwe elsewhere throughout this guide), 500 State Street. The museum is introduced this way.

> "Slow your pace, open your imagination, and encounter a people who, many years ago, lived in harmony with the sea and land. The sea and land gave them everything they needed to sustain life. In return they were grateful to the spirit of everything that was. Who were these people who occupied this land for thousands of years before the coming of Europeans? Step into their world. See how they lived and what they believed. Learn the teachings and traditions of the Anishnawbeeg people, whose way is practiced and preserved even today."

The Museum of Ojibwa Culture. Courtesy of Bob Royce.

Indoor and outdoor exhibits include a miniature longhouse and an eight-minute video that describes the sad saga of removing Native American children and moving them to government schools for education.

The gift store features a large selection of handmade Native American crafts and arts including sculpture, paintings, jewelry, beadwork, pill boxes, pottery, baskets, moccasins, and books.

The woman in charge of the museum was fascinating. One of the greatest joys of traveling to a laid-back, easy-going place like the U.P. is taking time to listen to and engage with locals.

Free guided tours of St. Ignace (tips gladly accepted). Tours start in front of the museum, then continue down the Boardwalk. For about 90 minutes you will hear stories of the Ojibwe, the settlers of the seventeenth and eighteenth centuries, and a history of St. Ignace.

• Beaches, Parks, and Trails

Bridge View Park, Boulevard Avenue, is a perfect site for a photo op. The majestic bridge looms in the background. The Wawatam lighthouse perches at the end of the boardwalk. This is not a real, honest-to-goodness lighthouse but a miniature that adds color or ornamentation. Park amenities include sheltered picnic tables, restrooms, and beautiful flowers.

Wawatam Lighthouse. Courtesy of Bob Royce.

<<>>

Civilian Conservation Corps (CCC) of Hiawatha National Forest. Visitors can experience nine different CCC sites in the Upper Peninsula including camps and a pine plantation. For information go online to the Hiawatha National Park Website at https://www.nationalforests.org/our-forests/find-a-forest/hiawatha-national-forest.

<<>>

Straits State Park, 720 Church Street, walking trails, campground, fire pits, and picnic areas.

<<>>

Mission Park. (See Museum of Ojibwa Culture which is located there.)

• Other Stops to Consider

Castle Rock, 2811 Mackinac Trail. The 207 steps offer exercise if you've been cramped in a car too long. A bonus is another spectacular view. Not a destination stop but an interesting pause in your journey. Rising nearly 200 feet above water level, the rock was once called Pontiac's Lookout.

You'll appreciate it more with a good set of binoculars.

Castle Rock.
Courtesy of Bob Royce.

<<>>

Chain Lake, Mile Marker 346 off I-75. You can debate whether this is a large pond or a small lake, but either way the fishing for rock bass, bullhead, sunfish, sucker, largemouth bass, perch, and northern pike is great.

<<>>

Mystery Spot, US 2 (at 150 Martin Lake Drive), five miles west of St. Ignace. Voted by readers of *Michigan Living* as the #1 unusual attraction in the state. What began as a spot to experience optical illusions that jiggle your stomach has grown to include a guided tour, 18-hole mini-golf course, and ziplining.

• LIGHTHOUSE

Wawatam Lighthouse. (See Bridge View Park in this section.)

• THE FAMOUS OR INFAMOUS WITH TIES TO ST. IGNACE

Prentiss Marsh Brown, a politician, was born June 18, 1889, in St. Ignace and attended public school there. He also practiced law and was a prosecuting attorney in his hometown before losing runs for the Michigan House of Representatives and the Michigan Supreme Court. He was elected the Democrat from Michigan's 11th Congressional District to the United States House of Representatives for the 73rd Congress and was reelected to the 74th Congress, where he served until November 1936 when he was elected to the U.S. Senate. During his tenure he advocated for the construction of the Mackinac Bridge and became known as the Father of the Mackinac Bridge. He lost his bid for re-election in 1942 and returned to St. Ignace. He died at the age of 84 and is buried at Lakeside Cemetery.

<<>>

Les Sweetland, professional baseball pitcher, was born in 1901 in St. Ignace. He pitched in the Major Leagues for four years (Philadelphia Phillies and Chicago Cubs) where poor performance finally ended his career and sent him to the farm system from which he never returned to his former glory.

ST. MARYS RIVER

The St. Marys River is one of three rivers that are part of Michigan's St. Lawrence Seaway; the others are the Detroit River and the St. Clair River. The St. Marys River connects Lake Huron with Lake Superior. The river runs 74.5 miles from Superior, with a fall of 23 feet, southeast into Huron. It is an international border between Michigan and Ontario, Canada. The river exits Lake Superior at Sault Ste. Marie, a twin city divided between the U.S. and Canada by the Sault Ste. Marie International Bridge. The St. Marys Rapids are just below Sault Ste. Marie.

The man-made Soo Locks opened the waterways to giant freighters. (See Sault Ste. Marie in this guide.) Before Europeans arrived, Native Americans fished the waters of the St. Marys. They traded in the area and portaged around the rapids which were too strong for canoe travel. The Ojibwe gave St. Marys the name *Baawitigong*, meaning "at the cascading rapids."

The first lock was completed in May 1855. Today, four parallel locks on the U.S. side of the river make water travel possible for big ships.

During World War II, heavy security guarded the waterway, and protection was further strengthened after the attack on Pearl Harbor in 1941. Through this river, 90% of the iron ore needed for the military effort was transported from the Upper Peninsula to plants in the lower part of Michigan.

3. DETOUR VILLAGE

At the far eastern tip of the Upper Peninsula is tiny DeTour Village with the most recent population statistic available of 318 (2017). Detour in French means the turn. The village marks the turning point for ships entering the channel connecting Lake Huron to the St. Marys River.

The first residents of DeTour were the Mascoutin, Odawa, and Ojibwe Native Americans who established encampments in the region long before European explorers, including Father Marquette, Louis Joliet, Antoine De La Cadillac, and Renĕ Robert Cavelier-sieur-de-La-Salle passed through. As a Native American settlement, it was called *Giwideonaning* which translated as "the point which we go around in a canoe."

DeTour was an integral part of the fur trade. It had a large Metis (French-Native American) population. The area was organized in 1850 as Warren Township named after its first postmaster, Ebenezer Warren. The name changed to DeTour when the second postmaster assumed the position. In 1899 it incorporated as a village designated as the Incorporated Village of DeTour.

• Museum

DeTour Passage Historical Museum, 104 Elizabeth Street, chronicles the history of the village, both its growth, and the struggles it faced over the years. Displayed are freighter artifacts and Captain's Quarters. The museum is also a location to obtain additional information about the community, and a place to view freighter traffic entering the St. Marys River.

• Beaches, Parks, and Trails

Albany Beach, nine miles from DeTour Village on Lake Huron, located on a pull-off of M-134 just east of M-48. If quiet is what you seek, this secluded beach is where you'll find it. You can walk down a narrow trail to the beach.

<<>>

Caribou Beach Lake. A small lake west of town that offers boating, fishing, kayaking, and swimming in the summer and ice fishing, skating, and snowmobiling in the winter.

<<>>

Malette Park on the St. Marys River at the edge of DeTour on M-134. Amenities include picnic tables, grills, public boat launch, kayak put-in spots, beach, and a place to relax and watch the river traffic.

<<>>

Shula Giddens Park, along the St. Marys River in DeTour attached to the south end of the Botanical Gardens (See Below.) From here you can swim to Frying Pan Island.

<<>>

The State Forest Campground, six miles from town on M-134, may have the best Lake Huron beaches in the area. Trails for walking.

<<>>

Locals also claim there is a **Bare Ass Beach**, but you'll have to find it on your own. All they'll divulge is it's along the shore near DeTour.

• Another Stop to Consider

DeTour Botanical Gardens, M-134 Scenic Highway in DeTour. Many stone-lined, cultivated areas along the shore. Each seems to be planted by a different person and displays distinct plants and decorations, many as memorials to departed loved ones. A peaceful place with benches to enjoy the flowers. Picnic area.

• LIGHTHOUSE

The Detour Reef Light. In the water, three miles south of DeTour. This automated light sits at the southern entrance of the DeTour Passage between the eastern end of Michigan's Upper Peninsula and Drummond Island. A passage made dangerous by shoals, boats must slip past a shallow area with a maximum depth of 23 feet. Originally the light was erected on the shore at Point DeTour. It was moved offshore to the reef in 1931.

• SHIPWRECK

The tug, ***General,*** sank a few miles above DeTour in November 1910 in a collision with the steamer *Athabasca.* Three lives were lost. The *General* remained on the bottom for nine years before being raised and put back into service for another ten years. In 1930 the *General* caught fire while docked at DeTour. The machinery aboard was salvaged, and then the hull was allowed to sink near Frying Pan Island.

4. THE ISLANDS OF THE ST. MARYS RIVER

Drummond, Neebish, and Sugar Island

Drummond Island, an outcropping of four-hundred-million-year-old limestone known as Engadine Dolomite, is a short ride from the dock at DeTour. In addition to ferries, there are flights from Sault Ste. Marie, Pellston, and Detroit to Drummond's small airport to get you there.

The auto ferry transports both you and your car. As you enter Drummond's harbor, you will see the quarry which has operated on the island since 1853. Drummond Island is the second-largest freshwater island in the U.S. and describes itself as Michigan's Ultimate Playground. If you love the outdoors, you may agree.

Drummond Island is a place to relax, listen to the haunting call of the loon, and enjoy life's simple pleasures. The island has 150 miles of rocky shoreline with coves waiting to be explored. Its 13 ecosystems offer homes to 160 species of birds. The habitats include six forest types and five swamp-marsh types as well as inland lakes and rivers and rocky beaches.

You can ride over 100 miles of ATV and ORV trails, kayak the Heritage Water Trail around the island, or scuba dive the final resting place of multiple shipwrecks.

Wildlife encounters may include deer, black bear, snowshoe hare, otter, fox, coyote, wolf, bobcat, and maybe even a moose or two. Harbor Island National Wildlife Refuge is located in Potagannissing Bay, a shallow, island-strewn bay, just northwest of Drummond Island. This 695-acre area became part of the National Wildlife Refuge system in 1983. A trail system is in progress to allow visitors to explore more closely the various habitats.

Drummond Island is a paradise for hunters, fishers, and photographers. There's a golf course for those seeking a more structured sport experience.

The stars may appear clearer than you've ever seen them. Sitting on your porch with a glass of wine, bottle of beer, or your favorite soft drink, you may decide you are as close to heaven as you can get before dying.

• Shipwrecks

Many ships have settled to the bottom of the St. Marys River near Drummond Island. They are a source of interest to divers and snorkelers. Many were abandoned and died of natural causes—lack of maintenance seems a common thread. Among those ships are steamer *Alice C*, steamer *Two Myrtles*, steamer *Superior*, steamer *John W. Cullen*, schooner barge *Delaware*, steamer *J.C. Ford*, steamer *E. J. Laway Jr.*, barge *Ste. Marie*, steamer *George H. Ely*, steamer *Agnes W*, tug *Silver Spray*, and schooner *John B. Merrill.* There is also a mystery ship with a nameplate that cannot be read.

<<>>

Neebish Island

There is no current reliable census information, but it is estimated the population hovers around 100 permanent residents or cottage owners. Located west of the international border that separates the United States from the Canadian province of Ontario, this 21.5-acre U.S. island is divided into two parts, Big Neebish and Little Neebish. The island sits in the St. Marys River, 25 miles southeast of Sault Ste. Marie, directly south of Sugar Island.

Europeans arrived in the early 1600s and may have made a stop on this island that was previously occupied only by Ojibwe, Odawa, and Bodawatomi (Potawatomie). The name given to the island by Europeans came from the Ojibwe word *aniibiish*, which means leaf.

Originally, the channel between the island and the Michigan mainland was navigable only by small craft, so the earliest settlements developed on the east side (nearest Michigan mainland) of the island on Little Neebish.

From 1877 to 1893, a private sawmill employing 150 men operated on the island near the creek between Big Neebish and Little Neebish.

Today, upbound traffic sailing around the island to Lake Superior passes the island's east side, while downbound traffic to Lake Huron passes through a deepened channel on the island's west side. Neebish is a remote place which may be its appeal. You won't stumble over an influx of tourists.

Ferry service from Sault Ste. Marie transports you to the island's tiny village of Barbeau that promotes its unique vantage point for watching freighter traffic as the giant ships exit the Rock Cut. The calm, protected water is perfect for kayaking and fishing. You may catch some of the tastiest walleye, perch, and bass in the Great Lakes.

• Movie with a Tie to Neebish Island

The Switch, a 2010 film starring Jennifer Aniston and Jason Bateman, referred to Neebish Island as the location of Roland Nilson's parents' cabin. Nilson is played by

Patrick Wilson. It's a pretty tenuous connection, but it's all there was.

<<>>

Sugar Island, population (2010) of 783, lies in the St. Marys River at the eastern tip of the Upper Peninsula between the U.S. and the Canadian province of Ontario. Also called Maple Sugar Island, it was known to Native Americans for its abundance of sugar maples from which they made maple syrup.

The island has a landmass of approximately 49 square miles and is accessed by auto ferry from Sault Ste. Marie.

The subject of a border dispute between the two countries, Sugar Island became part of the U.S. by treaty on August 9, 1842. An interesting trivia fact: In 1945 Sugar Island was nominated as a possible location for the headquarters of the United Nations.

Much of the island remains undeveloped, and the Bay Mills Indian Community and the Sault Ojibwe have interests on the island. For the Ojibwe, it is part of their ancestral homeland.

The University of Michigan Biological Station operates Chase Osborn Preserve near the southern tip of the island.

• The Famous or Infamous with a Tie to Sugar Island

Chase Osborn, 27th Governor of Michigan from 1911 to 1913, was named Chase Salmon after abolitionist Salmon Chase. Chase, in what might be called an understatement, is described as colorful, brilliant, and eccentric. After his term of governor, he traveled the world, then came back to Michigan and ran for another term as governor. He was defeated. In 1931 Chase and his wife Lillian legally adopted 37- year-old Stellanova Brunt, and Brunt changed her last name to Osborn. After Lillian died, Chase had the adoption

Chase Osborn, 1910. Public Domain.

of Stellanova annulled. In later years, Chase was confined to a wheelchair, and Stellanova became his nurse. On April 9, 1949, at Osborn's Georgia residence, he and Stellanova were married. He was 89, and she was 54. Two days later he died. His remains were interred at his Michigan residence on Sugar Island.

• Book with a Tie to Sugar Island

The Iron Hunter, by Chase Osborn, was first published in 1919 and republished in 2002. The book is autobiographical and describes the author's lifetime work including prospecting for iron ore in Michigan's Upper Peninsula. Clear from his writing is Osborn's love of the outdoors. Osborn wrote several other books and co-wrote some with his adopted daughter, Stellanova. She also wrote several books of poetry on her own. (See Famous with Ties to Sugar Island.) Perhaps Chase Osborn's autobiography unravels what sounds like an interesting and complicated relationship.

5. Sault Ste. Marie

In the mid-1800s, Henry Wadsworth Longfellow sat on the shore at Sault Ste. Marie. Captivated by the splendor of The Big Sea Shining Water, he found his inspiration for "Hiawatha."

The City of Sault Sainte Marie, on the northeastern tip of the Upper Peninsula, had a 2020 population of 13,434. Michigan's U.P. has a tad more than three percent of the entire state population. The Soo, as it is called, is the second-largest city in the U.P. Marquette is first. The city is much smaller than her twin city, Sault Ste. Marie, Ontario (population 73,368 in 2016), and the two cities are connected by the Sault Ste. Marie International Bridge. Sault Ste. Marie is 350 miles from downtown Detroit.

The name Sault Ste. Marie comes from the obsolete French word sault meaning a fall or rapid in a river. In this case a rapid in the St. Marys River.

The area was a fishing and trading crossroad for the Native Americans who had lived in the area for centuries before the arrival of Europeans. Jesuit Father Jacques Marquette heard about the village and traveled there in 1668 and founded a Catholic Mission. French fur traders established a trading post nearby. Originally a single community, it was governed by the French, then the British, before it was divided by the U.S.-British Joint Boundary Commission, which in 1817, fixed the border between the U.S. and the British Province of Upper Canada as the St. Marys River, creating the twin cities.

Shipping traffic was opened to the St. Marys River through the Soo Locks (See Other Stops to consider), which can accommodate ships 1,000 feet long and a smidgeon over 100 feet wide.

Freighter clearing the Soo Locks.
Courtesy of Bob Royce.

Sault Ste. Marie is host to the International 500 Snowmobile Race held in February. Snowfall is a way of life and Yoopers make the best of the 120 inches they average annually. December 1995 surpassed all expectations when in a five-day snowstorm 62 inches of snow fell—28 inches in one day alone.

• Museums

Tower of History, 326 East Portage. Take a quick elevator ride up 210 feet to the top where you'll find observation platforms from which to view the St. Marys River, the twin cities, the international bridge, and the surrounding countryside.

Tower of History.
Courtesy of Pixabay Free Images.

The Catholic church built the tower in 1968 as a shrine to history, and it was meant to be part of a larger complex that paid homage to Bishop Baraga (the snowshoe priest) and other well-known priests with ties to the area. The expansion never materialized, and the goal of a larger development was scrapped. The tower was donated to Sault Ste. Marie which operates it as the Tower of History. The current museum remains true to its original mission of telling the tale of the early missionaries, but its scope has widened to include local and Native American history. There is a video presentation on the lower-level exhibit area.

<<>>

Museum Ship Valley Camp, 501 East Water Street. Welcome aboard a retired freighter for a taste of ship life. You'll see the inside of the engine room, kitchen, sleeping quarters, pilothouse, and gain an appreciation for the history presented through pictures and artifacts in 20,000 feet of exhibit space. You can see local species of fish—walleye, perch, pike, and trout—in the four 1,200-gallon aquariums. There are also two lifeboats from the *Edmund Fitzgerald* and a film about her tragic demise. On deck you may get lucky and see a freighter passing through the locks.

<<>>

River of History Museum, 531 Ashmun. Lots of information packed into a small space. Some visitors walk through in a few minutes, others saturate themselves in the history and spend much longer. It's up to you. Murals and paintings augment your learning about the area. There is a video to make your experience more meaningful, plus hands-on exhibits.

• Beaches, Parks, and Trails

Bellevue Park, Queen Street East, has a play area with slides, swings, climbing structures, a splash pad for hot humid days, trails, a greenhouse, and a pavilion.

<<>>

Kinsman Park, 767 Landslide Road, has wide walking and bike trails with beautiful scenery and cascading falls. Nice place for a picnic on the grass.

<<>>

Pointe Des Chenes Beach, 57 Des Chenes Drive, offers picnic tables nestled in trees. Enjoy the water views and swimming beach. Restrooms with running water and changing rooms.

<<>>

Roberta Bondar Park, 65 Foster Drive, a sprawling park along the river. Nice place to walk and appreciate the views. The park honors Canada's first female astronaut.

<<>>

Sault Ste. Marie Boardwalk, along the St. Marys River. Perfect place for a stroll and people watching.

• Other Stops to Consider

The Soo Locks, 329 West Portage Avenue. This point of interest can justifiably be described as an international tourist site. Check in at the Visitors Center which provides you with an overview and history of the four locks—Poe, MacArthur, Davis, and Sabin. A working model of the locks is one of the interesting exhibits. More than 11,000 vessels, carrying as much as ninety million tons of cargo, pass through these locks every year. In the simplest of layperson's terms, the purpose of the locks is to allow great ships to equalize the drop into the St. Marys Falls from Lake Superior and get safely into the river on their downbound journey into Lake Huron. The grounds are a pleasant park-like setting. If you are in Sault Ste. Marie, it is worth stopping and seeing a magnificent example of man's ingenuity.

<<>>

Historic Water Street, between Johnston Street and Osborn Boulevard near the intersection of Water and Johnston. You can walk past the John Johnston House, Henry Rowe Schoolcraft's Indian Agency Office, Bishop Frederic Baraga's House, and the Kemp Coal Dock Office Museum.

Further west you can see the sites of Fort Brady, the first Jesuit Mission, and Fort de Repentigny, all of which were located in the block that includes City Hall. Two walls in the Historic area provide interpretive panels. It's an easy half-mile walk that comes with a history lesson.

Historic Water Street. Courtesy of Pixabay Free Images.

<<>>

For those interested, **Soo Locks Boat Tours** leave from Dock 2.

• Lighthouse

Pointe Aux Pins Range Lighthouse, Pointe Louise Drive, on the Ontario side of the St. Marys River, is best seen from a boat.

• The Famous or Infamous with Ties to Sault Ste. Marie

It is no surprise that the list of notables from or with ties to the Soo is heavily predominated by hockey stars or those connected to the sport: **Taffy Abel**, former Olympian and NHL player; **Cliff Barton**, former NHL player; **Jeff Blashill**, head coach of the NHL's Detroit Red Wings was born in Detroit but grew up in Sault Ste. Marie where his father was a professor at Lake Superior State University; **Bun LaPrairie**, former NHL player; **Tip O'Neill**, former NHL player; **Vic Desjardins**, former NHL player; and **Bruce Martyn**, radio and TV play-by-play announcer of the

Detroit Red Wings from 1964 to 1995, graduated from Lake Superior State University and began his radio career at WSOO.

<<>>

A second group of notables had ties to the fur trade. Their names are part of the area's history, and they are the patriarchs and matriarchs of the region. They include **John Johnston**, a Scotch-Irish immigrant and one of the first European settlers who came to the area in 1790. He married **Ozhaguscodaywayquay**, daughter of prominent chief, Waubojeeg. After marriage, Ozhaguscodaywayquay took the name Susan Johnston. The marriage between her and John was one of many alliances between fur traders and the Ojibwe. Another historically significant figure was **Henry Rowe Schoolcraft**, ethnographer and U.S. Indian agent who in his official capacity named several counties and places in Michigan. Schoolcraft married **Bamewawagezhikaquay** also known as Jane Johnston Schoolcraft, daughter of John and Susan Johnston. Both Henry and Jane were prominent writers of their time. Jane has been acknowledged as the country's first Native American literary writer. In 2009 she was inducted into the Michigan Women's Hall of Fame.

<<>>

A third group with neither a fur-trade nor hockey ties includes **Terry O'Quinn**, an actor best known for playing John Locke in the ABC series *Lost*. He later played Brian LeCroix in the *FBI Most Wanted*. He has many other TV and movie credits. O'Quinn was born in Sault Ste. Marie.

<<>>

Chase S. Osborn was Michigan's only governor from the Upper Peninsula. (See Osborn under the Famous or Infamous with Ties to Sugar Island.)

<<>>

Joseph H. Steere served as a justice in the Michigan Supreme Court from 1911 through 1927 and was Chief

Justice in 1913 and 1921. A practicing Quaker, he moved to Sault Ste. Marie in 1878 and resided there until his death in 1936.

• Book with a Tie to St. Ignace

Angeline Boulley, ***The Firekeepers Daughter*** (March 16, 2021 release). Boulley is an enrolled member of the Sault Ste. Marie Chippewa (referenced as Ojibwe elsewhere in this guide) Tribe. She is Bear Clan from Sugar Island and sets her debut novel in Sault Ste. Marie. The book provides a glimpse into Upper Peninsula life and also the complexities of Ojibwe culture. The author is garnering rave reviews for her story of 18-year-old Daunis Fontaine told in four parts, each representing one of the four directions of the Ojibwe medicine wheel teachings.

After witnessing a murder, Daunis finds her life splintered. She becomes a reluctant FBI informant. Her efforts to solve the crime and protect her tribe from a deadly methamphetamine epidemic often clash with her love for her family and her Anishinaabe heritage.

Boulley makes you see and taste and feel Daunis' world from its hockey craziness to its weather anomalies. It is hard to imagine a book that could give you a better sense of Michigan's Upper Peninsula.

This Young Adult crime thriller created a bidding war among 12 publishers. Henry Holt Books for Young Readers of Macmillan Publishers secured the release through a deal rumored to be seven figures. Barack and Michelle Obama's production company Higher Ground Productions is also exploring adapting the novel for a Netflix series, so stay tuned.

• Ghost Stories

The Ghost of the Nagging, Unfaithful Wife. In a Native American village near Sault Ste. Marie, there lived a hardworking man who fished and hunted from dawn to sunset to keep his wife and two sons fed. The wife was never satisfied with her husband's efforts and took advantage of every opportunity to berate him. She nagged and complained without letup. She began keeping company with other men. It was only a matter of time before the husband caught his wife in a compromising situation, and when it happened, he shot both the wife and her lover.

He was rid of her. No punishment for the murder could be worse than listening to the woman's constant criticism, thought the man. To his horror, there was something worse. His wife's ghost appeared to him and continued ranting. She may have been a complete ghost, but all he saw was her head and nonstop mouth. As though complaining to her mate wasn't enough, the woman appeared to her sons and accused them of siding with their father.

One day the sons sat alongside Superior's shore mending fish nets when their mother's ghost began her incessant grumbling. A beautiful crane walked the water's edge looking for dinner. The two boys asked the crane to take them away from the unpleasant situation. The crane agreed, and the boys climbed on the crane's back. The crane gave them one warning—do not touch my head. The boys were more than willing to abide by the restriction, and the crane flew them far away from their mother's tirade.

The mother's ghost-head saw what had happened. When the crane returned and resumed catching minnows along the water's edge, she demanded the bird carry her to her boys. The crane, unable to tolerate her whining, finally relented. The bird gave the woman the same warning it had given her sons. "Do not touch my head." The woman agreed. They soared into the clouds. The woman couldn't resist. No bird would tell her what to do. She touched the bird's head. Immediately the bird made a dive that shook the woman from its back. She splashed into the icy waters of the Great Lake and her ghost was never seen or—more importantly—heard from again.

Flying Crane. Courtesy of Pixabay Free Images.

<<>>

Other Soo Hauntings. The ghost of a former ship captain haunts the Soo Brewing Company where steps can be heard coming from the second floor when no one is there. Aboard the Museum Ship Valley Camp, a ghost is heard coughing as it shovels coal into the furnace. And, there are reports of the ghost of a former woman of easy virtue still inhabiting Antler's Restaurant where she had earned her living when it was a brothel.

LAKE SUPERIOR

On the shores of Gitche Gumee,
Of the shining Big-Sea-Water,
Stood Nokomis, the old woman,
Pointing with her finger westward,
O'er the water pointing westward,
To the purple clouds of sunset.
Song of Hiawatha, Henry Wadsworth Longfellow

She is Michigan's Shining Big Sea Water. She is also the biggest, baddest, deepest, coldest, and clearest of the five Great Lakes. In fact, she is the largest freshwater sea in the world with 31,700 square miles of surface area, approximately the size of Maine. She has a maximum depth of 1,333 feet which is deeper than the Empire State Building is tall. There is enough water in Superior to cover the landmasses of North and South America with a foot of water, and she has 2,726 miles of shoreline if you include her islands. She borders the northern coast of Michigan's Upper Peninsula. She is an unapparelled beauty and a force of nature rolled into a natural resource of immense proportion. During her famous storms of November, waves of 20 feet are normal. Waves of 30 feet are not unusual.

The French first called her *la lac superieur* to indicate her position as the upper lake. The English translated that to the superior lake. Perhaps it was a well-made change since it is an apt description. The Ojibwe called her *Kitchigami* which translates as great lake, so it appears the names by which she was first called reflect the awe man had for this body of water.

A word of advice before you travel Lake Superior's coastline. Michigan's natural areas have mosquitoes. They are called skeeters and often referred to as the state bird. These are not just any mosquitoes. If you go for a morning walk along any woodsy or grassy trails, they will find you.

You may not see the minuscule, blood-sucking, good-for-nothing, dive bombers. They hide in the morning dewy grass and see your naked ankles as breakfast. You'll start scratching . . . and scratching . . . and scratching. If you are a native Michigander and have suffered mosquito bites as the price you pay to live in this water wonderland, you may be able to ignore the bites. They may not swell up to the size of golf balls and drive you mad. Humans may develop a degree of tolerance to the insidious bites. However, if you are not used to being bitten, you may rush to the doctor to find the source of this major outbreak of oversized hives. The doctor will smile and kindly explain, "It isn't what you've been eating, but what's been eating you." Consider yourself warned.

You can become intimate with Superior's four sister lakes. In hot summer months, they seduce you, entice you to swim and frolic in their waves. Superior remains aloof—standoffish. Her chill waters seldom inviting.

There's an old tale that if you seek a spot to bury a body, Superior's your place. The bacteria feeding on a sunken decaying corpse generate gas inside the body which causes it to float to the surface after a few days. But Lake Superior's water is cold year-round—rarely rising to 40 degrees and lower than that at its depths—so it inhibits decay. With waters never warm enough for decomposition, the body stays hidden. Gordon Lightfoot references this in the "Wreck of the Edmund Fitzgerald" when he sings, "The Lake it is said, never gives up her dead." None of the 29 who died in that most famous of shipwrecks have ever been brought up. (See Shipwrecks under Paradise and the Shipwreck Museum at Whitefish Point.)

Humans are estimated to have arrived 10,000 years ago after the glaciers of the last ice age receded. Native Americans had lived along Lake Superior for centuries before the arrival of Europeans in the 1600s.

Etienne Brule, an interpreter for Samuel Champlain, and Grenoble (first name not documented), lived among the original people learning their languages and customs. From the Huron tribe, these Europeans heard of another vast lake that perched above Lac du Huron. It was described as a lake that emptied into Huron by a waterfall and a river. The rapids were named for the king's brother, the Sault de Gaston. The falls, river, and lake were included on an early map published by Champlain in 1632.

Oddly, Superior was the second of the Great Lakes discovered by Europeans. The first was Huron. Explorers avoided the area of Erie and Ontario because they feared the native people living near those lakes. Lake Michigan was further inland in the chain.

Superior has the highest elevation of the five great lakes. It is an important cog in the Great Lakes Waterway system. Iron ore and other mined materials used in manufacturing as well as grains fill the freighters traveling across Superior, through the Soo Locks, up and down the St. Marys River, and into Lakes Huron and Michigan on their journey to far destinations. Shipping closes down when the lakes freeze over.

The southern shore of Lake Superior between Grand Marais and Whitefish Point has been called the Graveyard of the Great Lakes.

More than 80 species of fish are found in Superior, but the lake produces fewer dissolved nutrients and in turn fewer fish than the other Great Lakes. Overfishing and the introduction of foreign species such as the sea lamprey have factored in the decline of its fish population.

Rock Hunting in Lake Superior

Hunting for pudding stones along Huron and Drummond Island is easy. They may not be numerous, but once you see one, it's pretty clear what it is. Beach glass? Even the youngest children can spot this treasure. Petoskey stones are easily identifiable.

Agates. They won't look like this on the beach.
Courtesy of Pixabay Free Images.

Agates—those elusive treasures from Superior's shores—are tougher. True agates (if you should be so lucky) are hard to tell from imposters. The best way to prepare is to buy a guide to the many types of agates. Study it before you head out. You may want to take a spray bottle because the markings of wet agates are easier to recognize. You can dip your finds in Superior, but the shoreline is rocky and the water brutally cold.

6. Point Iroquois Light Station
(Including Hiawatha National Forest)

Point Iroquois Light Station. Courtesy of Pixabay Free Images.

Traveling the Lake Superior shoreline between Brimley and Whitefish Point on the south tip of Whitefish Bay, you'll come to the Point Iroquois Light Station, one of the oldest lighthouses guiding ships along the Lake Superior shoreline. The onsite volunteer staff is a repository of information about the history of the lighthouse and the area. The lighthouse was named for a famous 1662 battle in which the local Ojibwe, or Original People of the area, defeated their Iroquois enemy at this spot.

The grounds of the lighthouse are perfectly maintained. The interior Captain's Quarters are restored with period furniture. The climb to the top of the tower rewards you with a panoramic view of the Bay—often with freighters traveling in the distance.

Being the keeper of the light took a special kind of person. The demanding job required attention both day and night. Before being electrified, a large kerosene lamp provided the light source. Keepers refilled the lamp with oil every four hours. The lens had to be kept clean from soot, and the wick needed constant trimming. Point Iroquois was a plum assignment. The house was big enough for the head keeper and two assistants along with families to help shoulder the responsibility of safely guiding big ships through this dangerous patch of water.

You can walk the shoreline and look for agates and other natural treasures. The pathway to the water has benches where you can sit and soak in the beauty as you revel in the surroundings. The lighthouse was placed on the National Register of Historic Places in 1975. A giftshop is on premises.

• Museum

History Museum of Bay Mills & Brimley (Wheels of History Train Museum), 6749 South M-221. A pre-1905 passenger car and caboose house this small museum which includes artifacts of area railroads, early telephones, logging, fishing, and Bay Mills history. A gift shop is in the caboose. Seasonal.

• Beaches, Parks, and Trails

Hiawatha National Forest covers 894,836 acres in the Upper Peninsula and is divided into two units, eastside and westside. The forest touches more than 100 miles of shoreline, and both westside and eastside meet Lakes Superior and Michigan. The eastside unit of the forest reaches shoreline on Lake Huron. The forest has six wilderness areas and provides numerous camping opportunities. It is habitat for white-tailed deer, golden eagles, black bears, moose, coyotes, bobcats, bald eagles, beaver, red fox, Canadian lynx, hawks, and many other wildlife species.

• Shipwreck

S.S. Myron. Even with the lighthouse beacon to help navigation, the *S.S. Myron*, a wooden steamship, succumbed to one of the vicious Storms of November when the waves came cussing, and crashing, sputtering and surging. Built in 1888, the ship enjoyed a 31-year-career towing lumber barges before she sank in 1919. The crew perished, but the captain survived and was found clinging to wreckage. The *Myron* was towing the *Miztec* which made it through.

The *Myron* defied the commonly held belief that Superior never gives up her dead. In the days following the tragedy, all the deceased were found frozen in their lifejackets. Residents chopped corpses free from their icy sepulchers and sent the bodies to a local undertaker who buried them in Mission Hill Cemetery in Bay Mills Township.

Many of the *Myron*'s artifacts were illegally removed from the wreck site. They were recovered by the State of Michigan and are on loan, displayed at the Great Lakes Shipwreck Museum. (See Great Lakes Shipwreck Museum under Whitefish Point.)

The skeleton of the *S.S. Myron* is part of the Whitefish Point Underwater Preserve.

7. Whitefish Point

The Lake Superior shoreline along Whitefish Bay provides one photo op after another as you drive its 20 miles of national scenic byway.

Tourists come for more than the view. They come to visit the Whitefish Point Lighthouse, the Whitefish Point Bird Observatory, and the world-famous Whitefish Point Shipwreck Museum.

• Museum

The Whitefish Point Shipwreck Museum. *Money Magazine* dubbed it one of the best small museums in America. Numerous other accolades confirm it is a special place to visit.

Lake Superior around Whitefish Point is one of the most treacherous shipping channels in the Great Lakes earning it the unflattering and harsh nickname "Graveyard of the Great Lakes." The museum dedicates its existence to making shipwreck legends come to life. Through artifacts and exhibits, you piece together the stories of vessels and sailors who braved Superior's wrath, too many of whom didn't live to tell about their experience. The video theatre provides a short film documenting the sinking of the *Edmund Fitzgerald* and the efforts that raised her bell and made it part of the museum.

The museum store has a selection of lighthouse gifts, art, and books for those interested in maritime history and shipwrecks.

• Another Stop to Consider

Whitefish Point Bird Observatory. More than 300 species of birds have been recorded at the observatory. You may spot songbirds, raptors, shorebirds, and water birds from the observation deck. The land and water features of Whitefish Point create a natural corridor that attracts thousands of birds during spring and fall migrations. The flocks use the area as a stopover habitat to replenish their energy before continuing across Superior. The migrations are not only opportunities for observation but a chance to enhance education, research, and conservation. Among the species that migrate are golden eagles, peregrine falcons, and boreal owls. The area has been a nesting site for the federally endangered piping plover.

• Light Station

Whitefish Point Light Station marks the southeastern end of Lake Superior's Shipwreck Coast which stretches west to Munising. This dangerous part of the lake has claimed over 550 ships. More than a third of those lie on the bottom near Whitefish Point at the critical juncture where they entered or left Superior.

Whitefish Point Light Station. Courtesy of Bob Royce.

In 1849 the lighthouse first sent its beacon light into the fog of the night, and it has remained in operation ever since, making it the oldest operating lighthouse on Lake Superior. The site was added to the National Register of Historic Places in 1973. The Whitefish Point Underwater Preserve protects many of the shipwrecks which are available to sport divers. The lighthouse is open seasonally for visitors.

• Shipwrecks

The legend lives on from the Chippewa on down
of the big lake they call Gitche Gumee.

The ***S.S. Edmund Fitzgerald***, immortalized by Gordon Lightfoot in his ballad, "The Wreck of the Edmund Fitzgerald," remains alive in the imaginations of Michiganders nearly a half century after she sank.

When launched in 1958, the *Mighty Fitz* at 729 feet (more than the length of 2½ football fields) was the largest freighter on the lakes. She spent her working days hauling iron ore from mines near Duluth, Minnesota, to manufacturers in Detroit, Michigan, and Toledo, Ohio. As strong and vital as she was, this *Titanic of the Great Lakes* was no match when the Witch of November came calling. On November 10, 1975, the *Fitzgerald* succumbed to Superior's immense rage. What took her down remains a mystery, although the weather and 35-foot waves played roles.

The captain radioed a last message that he had a serious problem, was listing, had lost his radar, and the storm was coming for him. That night, the frenzied hurricane hurled 29 men to their watery grave. Not a single body was recovered. A 1994 expedition of divers to the wreck found a body, fully-clothed, face down in the sediment near the bow of the ship. The deceased was left undisturbed where he lay. Some critics felt the remains should have been brought up to give the family closure. With modern technology, retrieval should be possible for at least some of the bodies still down there. The families opposed bringing them up. They know where their loved ones are and feel that closure is not an issue. They don't want the dead torn from their final resting place in the company of the crewmates with whom they shared their tragic last minutes.

It is believed that if the *Fitzgerald* could have made another 15 miles, she'd have survived. That's how close she was to the protection of Whitefish Bay.

The Edmund Fitzgerald.
Courtesy of Pixabay Free Images.

8. Upper and Lower Tahquamenon Falls

While not on the shoreline of Lake Superior, this is a stop for which it is worth traveling inland a few miles. From Paradise, drive west on M-123 (Lower Falls Road) 11 miles until you see the signs for the falls. The upper and lower falls are two separate falls on the Tahquamenon River. They are about four miles apart, and you can drive between them.

Tahquamenon Falls. Courtesy of Bob Royce.

Park rangers are often asked whether the falls are polluted. The reason for the question is the brown color of the water. The simple answer is "No, the color is not related to pollution." The explanation is that tannins leached from adjacent cedar swamps are drained by the river causing the color. The distinct golden coppery color is so noticeable that it has given rise to the nickname, Rootbeer Falls.

The upper falls are more than 200 feet across with a drop of about 48 feet. During the spring runoff, the river drains as much as 50,000 gallons of water per second.

Downstream, the lower falls are a series of smaller falls that cascade around an island. You can reach the island by rowboat, and a hiking trail connects the falls along the riverside. The lower falls, if not swimmable, are an appropriate place to cool off on a hot day.

• A Park

The Tahquamenon Falls State Park follows the Tahquamenon River as it passes over the Tahquamenon Falls and drains into Whitefish Bay. The park offers 46,179 acres making it Michigan's second-largest state park.

Mostly undeveloped, the park has 22 miles of hiking trails, five campgrounds, and 350 campsites.

• Book with a Tie to Tahquamenon Falls

Henry Wadsworth Longfellow's 1855 epic poem, "The Song of Hiawatha," is set in Michigan's Upper Peninsula and includes a line stating that Hiawatha built his canoe "by the rushing Tahquamenaw."

9. Crisp Point Lighthouse

This gem may be the highlight of your trip to the U.P. One of the original four Lake Superior Light Saving Stations, the Crisp Point Lighthouse was first proposed in 1896, approved in 1902, and became operational in 1904. It stands 14 miles west of Whitefish Point but don't assume it's a quick drive.

Hidden deep in forested lands, getting to the lighthouse—arriving at that opening where the lake looms ahead—may prove a testament to your determination. You better be driving a four-wheel utility vehicle. No Mercedes, tiny Miata, or sissy car should attempt the trip.

Author enjoying the solitude. Courtesy of Bob Royce.

Follow lighthouse signs from M-123. Bumpy roads may force you to consider turning around at several junctions. This is not a well-marked route. You will come to stops where you are unsure which way to go. Each time, convince yourself to push on. There are bears in the woods around you. You may not see them, but they will be watching you. They are short, close to the ground, and you may think they are just another tree stump. From the treed (or bear-infested) darkness that envelops you, you will finally break out into brilliant sunlight. You are there.

Where is there? A remote Superior shoreline, and if you are lucky, you have the destination to yourself. It is probably the first and only lighthouse where you can open the door and let yourself in. Or where there is a sign telling you to close the door behind you when you leave. You may be the sole soul climbing the tower or scootching out the small entry to the catwalk around the top of the lighthouse. If good fortune smiles on you, you can sit awhile, appreciate the view, and enjoy the tranquility with no one to disturb you.

Lighthouse lovers are lucky the Crisp Point Light remains standing. Vandalism and the elements nearly caused its demise. Dedicated volunteers poured many hours into restoration to keep this piece of history alive. The outbuildings are gone. In 1998 a thousand cubic yards of stone were placed along the shoreline to help slow erosion, and more stone has been added in several of the years since then. Plans for further stabilization will be carried out as funds become available.

Crisp Point Light.
Courtesy of Bob Royce.

The light is named for Christopher Crisp, one of its colorful keepers. There is a visitor center on the property, a small portion of which is a gift shop. The knowledgeable volunteers will share the history of the lighthouse. Restrooms are available. You can access the rocky Superior beach to search for agates.

• Shipwrecks

The freighter ***S.S. D.M. Clemson*** disappeared without a trace on December 1, 1908, somewhere between Crisp Point and Grand Marais. She was last seen leaving the Soo Locks headed into Superior. All twenty-four men aboard went down with her. The circumstances of the tragedy remain a mystery.

<<>>

The ***William Nottingham*** lost three men near Crisp Point lighthouse during the ferocious storm of 1913. The three crewmen boarded a lifeboat to fetch help. But the lifeboat overturned, and the men drowned.

10. Grand Marais

Grand Marais is located in Alger County which has 5,049 square miles and less than 10,000 residents. That's about two people per square mile. Grand Marais has a population of less than 500 and is one of the few places where men outnumber women.

The name is French. Grand means big or great, but what isn't clear is why the French use the word Marais to mean both a marsh and a harbor of refuge. It was one of five lifesaving stations established between Munising and Whitefish Point. A breakwater extends from the bay into Lake Superior where the Grand Marais Outer Range Light is located and still operational.

A small town without huge revenues, the city often struggled and argued among its residents over costs of dredging the harbor and keeping the light functional. The breakwater suffered significant damage due to neglect. The problem received some additional funding in a creative way. In 2011 *Reader's Digest* sponsored a contest called "We Hear You America." This contest provided visitors to the magazine's website a chance to express their support for their community and win not only kudos but cash. Grand Marais got more "cheers" (votes) than any other community, earning $40,000 and some attention for its plight.

Grand Marais is the eastern gateway to Pictured Rocks National Lakeshore.

• Museums

The former **United States Coast Guard Lifesaving Station**, E22030 Coast Guard Point, is at the west entrance to Grand Marais Harbor. The lifesaving station now serves as a ranger station and museum. The original light was built and became operational in 1899. In 1919 the lifesaving station was the site of a dramatic rescue. A crew of 17 was stranded aboard the steam barge *H.E. Runnels* in a wicked November storm. The *Runnels* was hauling a load of coal downlake when the weather turned precarious. The captain couldn't maneuver the narrow channel of the bay. He tried to back into the waves but suffered the loss of his steering gear. The broken wreck lies buried deep in the sand. The crew was rescued, but the feat required four trips through the angry lake.

The ranger station was originally across the road from its current location and faced the harbor. The current ranger station houses the Grand Marais Maritime Museum in its converted keeper's quarters. It displays artifacts from the lifesaving station including a medal awarded to a station crew member for the *Runnels* rescue.

<<>>

The **Pickle Barrel House**, northeast corner of Lake and Randolph Streets, is a two-part, two-story cabin built like no other you are likely to see. It was commissioned by

Pickle Barrel House.
Courtesy of Pixabay Free Images.

William Donahey as a surprise for his wife. The pickle-barrel-shaped structure was originally located in the woods at Grand Sable Lake. The design is based on a cartoon strip. (See The Famous or the Infamous with Ties to Grand Marais.) The larger of the two barrels is 16 feet high with the living room on the main floor and the bedroom upstairs. The smaller barrel was the kitchen. The two barrels were connected by a pantry. The Donaheys got so much attention from curiosity seekers that it became burdensome. After a decade, they gave up the cottage.

In 1936 the Pickle Barrel House was moved to downtown Grand Marais. It was recast as an ice cream stand, an information center, and then a souvenir shop before it fell into disrepair. In 2003 the Grand Marais Historical Society acquired the property and began restoration. Two years later the structure opened to the public. The museum features photos from the Donaheys' cottage years and William Donahey's artwork and cartoon strips as well as books.

<<>>

The Gitche Gumee Agate and History Museum, E21739 Brazel Street, is a place to learn about rocks and rock hunting and maybe buy the agates you couldn't find along the beach. This museum has been around for decades. Ownership has changed, but it remains dedicated to educating folks about geology, rock collecting, and displaying beautiful agates. The hours are seasonal and change by the day. Check the internet or call if this stop is important to you.

Agate Museum.
Courtesy of Bob Royce.

• Beaches, Parks, and Trails

Muskallonge Lake State Park is located 16 miles east of Grand Marais. It provides 217 acres of public recreation area with swimming and fishing, a 159-site campground, boat launch, picnic area, playground, and trails for hiking and snowmobiling.

<<>>

Sable Falls, H-58 west of Grand Marais, is located in the eastern portion of Pictured Rocks National Lakeshore. Water plunges 75 feet over sandstone formations. Stairs access the falls. There is a boardwalk between the minor falls and the upper (major) falls. The falls are not handicap accessible.

• Other Stops to Consider

Log Slide Overlook, Alger County Road H-58, Grand Marais. Miles of towering dunes. Perfect place for magnificent photos. You may want to walk down the bank, but what takes you a few minutes to descend can take an hour to climb back to where you started. Consider carefully before you slide down to the lakeshore. As you stand at the top of this sandy cliff area, think about the early logging companies that slid logs down this steep, sandy embankment to Lake Superior.

• Shipwrecks

The ***South Shore***, a small passenger and freight steamer, was put out of commission by a November storm. Her captain kept her offshore, hoping to survive the storm long enough to enter the harbor, but she filled with water. The crew from the lifesaving station rescued all aboard. The *South Shore* and her cargo were a total loss. Her remains lie five miles east of Grand Marais. The boiler can be seen, but the hull only appears intermittently depending on the shifting sand near the Log Slide.

<<>>

The ***Nirvana*** and the ***Galatea***, two wooden barges, sank west of the piers at Grand Marais in an early season, October 20, 1905, storm. Both ships were towed in consort by the *L.L.Barth.*

Consort is a nautical term for unpowered Great Lakes vessels, usually a fully loaded schooner or steamer barge, towed by a larger steamer. Often the larger steamer tows more than one schooner or barge at the same time. The consort system was used in the Great Lakes from the 1860s until around 1920.

In the case of the *Nirvana* and *Galatea*, the 65 miles an hour gale winds got the upper hand, and as the ships approached the harbor, the towline broke. Both the *Nirvana* and the *Galatea* were beached losing their entire cargoes. Pieces of these ships are buried in the sand.

<<>>

The ***H.E. Runnels*** (See United States Coast Guard Lifesaving Station Museum). The wreck lies broken and scattered and buried in the sand.

<<>>

The ***Hunter*** was built to be an ocean-going fish tug, but her owners redirected her to Lake Superior to haul fish and passengers. She burned in the Grand Marais harbor on October 4, 1904.

<<>>

The ***Manhattan***, an early screw steamer and passenger ship, had sunk and been raised three times prior to September 2, 1859, when she went down for a final time. She lies inside the harbor at Grand Marais.

<<>>

The ***Saveland***, a three-masted schooner used as a tow barge for coal and ore, was driven into an old pile dike after separating from her consort string in a heavy storm in 1903. Her cargo, 800,000 board feet of pine, was a total loss. Portions of the wreck sometimes peek through the sand of their burial spot.

• Lighthouse

The **Au Sable Light** remains an active lighthouse along the Pictured Rocks National Lakeshore west of Grand Marais off H-58. The Au Sable Light Station was built in 1874 on Au Sable Point, a hazardous stretch of the "Shipwreck Coast" feared for its shallow ridge of sandstone that lurks just below the surface and extends a mile into Lake

Superior. During early shipping days before navigational positioning, the main means of staying on course was keeping land in sight. Ship captains worried about turbulence caused by storms, thick fogs caused by cold lake air colliding with warm air from the sands, and unseen underwater hazards.

The lighthouse tower and attached keeper quarters were designed by Colonel Orlando Poe who was responsible for eight lighthouses that are known as Poe style structures. Poe was an army officer and engineer during the Civil War. He was part of William Tecumseh Sherman's march to the sea. After his military career, he turned to lighthouse construction on the Great Lakes. His designs were unique in location, materials, methods, hardships, and costs. The towers are white brick conical with black lanterns.

The Au Sable Light has a red brick lightkeeper's house next to the tower. The keeper's house has been renovated, and there is a visitor center on the lower floor. The upper floor provides an apartment for volunteer caretakers. The lighthouse tower is open to the public.

The Au Sable Light Station is on the National Register of Historic Places.

• The Famous or Infamous with Ties to Grand Marais

William Donahey was an author, illustrator, and cartoonist best known for his "Teenie Weenie" cartoon strips that were widely syndicated after their debut in the *Chicago Tribune* in 1914. The newspaper published the strips for 50 years. Donahey was introverted and shy. He turned to the solitary world of writing as a passion. He married another author, Mary Dickerson, for whom he built the very unusual Pickle Barrel House. (See Museums.) The couple spent summers near Grand Marais.

11. Munising

Munising, the county seat of Alger County, had a 2020 population of 2,197. Exuding small town charm along with its hearty welcome, Munising is located along the southern shoreline of Lake Superior in the heart of Hiawatha National Forest. Residents of the area know how to enjoy the unspoiled beauty of each season.

Spring is a time of renewal and promise as the world turns lush green. Budding flowers and singing birds announce their return to walkers along the trails.

Summer is easy to love as beaches beckon. The rivers and lake invite you to launch a canoe or a kayak, pack a picnic basket, and head to an adventure.

Fall is more temperamental, but the brilliant reds, oranges, yellows, and magentas displayed by the forests make it worth hiking or biking the many paths that wind through the region.

Winter means snowmobiling, cross-country skiing, and ice climbing. You'll be happy to have your cellphone for pictures. For all seasons but winter, make sure you pack abundant supplies of bug spray.

In the early 1800s, an Ojibwe village was located at the mouth of the Anna River where Munising now stands, but the encampment was moved to Sand Point. Munising was founded in 1850 and soon consisted of thirty homes, a blacksmith, a sawmill, and a lighthouse.

The Ojibwe word *minisiing* means at the island and is considered the origin of the town's name. It was renamed Gogarnville in 1889 when Julius Gogarn, a German-born American Civil War veteran, was appointed postmaster. Gogarn moved the post office to his farm where he carried out his duties for four years. After his tenure, the city restored the name Munising.

Munising prides itself on its natural enticements enhanced by the lake, rivers, forests, and 15 waterfalls including Alger Falls, Au Train Falls, Bridal Veil Falls, Chapel Falls, Horseshoe Falls, Laughing Whitefish Falls, Memorial Falls, Miners Falls, Munising Falls, Scott Falls, Spray Falls (front cover photo by Tim Trombley at grlksphot@charter.net), Tannery Falls, and Wagner Falls.

• Museums

Alger County Heritage Center, 1496 Washington Street, is located in an old schoolhouse. There are woodworking exhibits, photos, antiques, a fur trapper cabin behind the museum, and a friendly staff knowledgeable about the area's history. A gift shop offers books, art, postcards, and jewelry. This is a small museum that can be explored in less than an hour. It doesn't provide the reason for a day trip, but if you are in Munising, it is a worthwhile addition to your schedule.

<<>>

Pictured Rocks Interpretive Center, 100 West Munising Avenue, uphill from the Pictured Rocks Cruise Dock, features displays about the history and geology of the Pictured Rocks National Lakeshore. At the information desk, visitors obtain advice and maps for hiking and sightseeing. A short film about the Pictured Rocks helps orient you to how mother nature created this spectacular wonder.

• Beaches, Parks, and Trails

AuTrain Beach, eight miles west of Munising at the yellow flashing light in AuTrain. This is a popular roadside beach with the AuTrain River running into it. Since the river warms up more quickly than chilly Lake Superior, many visitors prefer swimming in the river. Your camping experience can include boating, fishing, canoeing, birdwatching, hiking, biking, or just relaxing with a good book or new friends you've met at the campground. The campsites include16 furnished safari tents, 11 furnished yurts, two grand yurts, two large furnished tipis, and three furnished mini-tipis. All sites have firepits, outdoor charcoal grills, and a picnic table. Restrooms and showers onsite.

<<>>

Chapel Beach, 15 miles east of Munising on H-58, five miles north to the end of Chapel Road, then a two-mile hike from the parking lot to Lake Superior. Named by early explorers as La Chapelle, this formation is one of the many interesting rock structures found throughout the Pictured Rocks National Lakeshore.

<<>>

Miners Falls, H-58 to Miners Castle Road, then follow signs. It's northeast of Munising. Miner's River is the water source of this 50-foot waterfall. From where you park, it is a short easy walk of less than a mile to beautiful views. There is a small platform from which you can take photos. You must stay on the paved trail, and pets are not permitted.

<<>>

Pictured Rocks National Lakeshore, located along 15 miles of Lake Superior shoreline around Munising. Depending upon the season, you can snowmobile, hike, bike, cross country ski, boat, fish, camp, or swim. Pictured Rocks derives its name from the colorful sandstone of the cliffs that reach up to 200 feet above lake level. The elements have sculptured the rocks into a variety of shallow caves, arches, and formations resembling castle turrets and human profiles.

The U.S. Congress designated Pictured Rocks the first National Lakeshore in the United States in 1966. It is governed by the National Park Service

Pictured Rocks Lakeshore. Courtesy of Pixabay Free Images.

<<>>

Sand Point Beach, 4.2 miles east of Munising, sheltered by the bay with shallow waters and fewer waves, is a perfect place to sun and swim. Warmest (remember, in Superior, warm is a relative term) water in the area. There are picnic tables on the sand. Restrooms available. The fine pinkish sand and crystal-clear waters with a treed backdrop offer plenty of photo opportunities.

<<>>

Wagner Falls, M-94 west of M-28, just outside of Munising. The falls are an easy walk from the parking lot to the viewing areas.

• Other Stops to Consider

Grand Island is part of the Hiawatha National Forest and a designated National Recreation Area. Located in Lake Superior one-half mile from Munising, it is accessible by ferry. To reach the Ferry dock, drive west on M-28, turn right (north) on Powell Point Road at the Welcome sign for Grand Island NRA, and proceed to the Ferry Service parking lot at Powell Point.

You may also use your personal watercraft (not jet skis) to reach the island. You will cross the Grand Island channel to Williams Landing at the southern tip of the island. Weather can be dicey, and crossing can be hazardous.

Grand Island is 13,500 acres of unspoiled, primitive beauty surrounded by Michigan's largest lake. It is perfect for nature enthusiasts, but the number of tourists allowed to visit the island annually is limited, and those who go will need reservations. There are no paved roads, but rather there are two-track gravel roads and single-track trails for mountain biking and hiking.

Your efforts to visit Grand Island will be rewarded by a vast smorgasbord of activities that includes hiking, bicycling, kayaking, paddle boarding, parasailing, camping, fishing, swimming, ice-climbing, birdwatching, wildflower viewing, and once-in-a-lifetime vistas from 300-foot cliffs. If you want to sit on a white sand beach and let your mind wander, that's fine too.

There are inland lakes, hardwood forests, marshes, dunes, extraordinary ecological features like Trout Bay's tombolo (sandy isthmus), caves, and Jacobsville and Munising sandstone cliffs. Added to the natural beauty is a fascinating history that began long before the first European fur traders came to the island in the early 1800s.

Vault toilets and drinking water are onsite, but you are well-advised to take at least your first supply of water with you. Shops and stores are absent on the island. There are 19 individual campsites and two group campsites on the island. At the time this travel book was written, there was also random camping allowed.

• Lighthouses

The Grand Island East Channel Lighthouse, slightly north of Munising, was put into service in 1868. It was hard to see and wasn't a reliable navigational tool, so it was replaced by the Munising Front and Rear Range Lights that are currently in service.

East Channel Lighthouse. Courtesy of Pixabay Free Images.

The neglected East Channel Lighthouse fell into disrepair, and almost washed away due to erosion. Funds were raised for its preservation, and today it stands in rustic form (not its original pristine condition) and is one of the most photographed lighthouses on the lakes.

<<>>

The Munising Front and Rear Range Lights were established in 1907 to work in tandem to guide ships safely through the open waters of Lake Superior, into the East Channel next to Grand Island, and then safely into the Munising Harbor. These matching lights replaced the Grand Island East Channel Light which had proven ineffective. The Front Range Light is located at the western edge of Munising north of M-28. It is managed by the National Park Service. The grounds of both lights are open to the public, but the towers are closed.

<<>>

The Grand Island Harbor Range Lights, also known as the Bay Furnace Lights, were put into service in 1867 but are currently inactive. They are located along the water's edge. A hiking trail leads you to the lights for easy viewing.

• Shipwrecks

The Alger Underwater Preserve was created by the State of Michigan to protect and preserve the underwater resources of the Pictured Rocks National Lakeshore. The shipwrecks of this area are better preserved than in most other underwater areas because they are less impacted by population and industry. It is the undisturbed quality of the shipwrecks that has drawn both academians and divers to the preserve. State law protects the ships in this area, making it illegal to carry away, alter, or destroy any property on the bottom of the Great Lakes.

The bones of sunken ships aren't all that await the intrepid diver in the Alger Underwater Preserve. Miners Castle, Ferry Dock Landing Drop-off, Cathedral Caves, Pancake Rocks, and other unique rock formations and caves invite exploration. Divers often find themselves in the company of large fish, and the reflection of sun shining into the water provides amazing color displays.

<<>>

The ***Bermuda***, a wooden canal schooner, is located in 20 feet of water in Grand Island's Murray Bay. Three crewmen lost their lives in the wreck that on October 15, 1870, took the ship and her cargo of 488 tons of iron ore to the bottom.

<<>>

The ***Elma***, a 160-foot schooner-barge, wrecked on September 26, 1895, about two miles from Miners Castle. The wreck sustained only one casualty from the 11 aboard. Shifting sand often leaves the entire bottom of the ship visible.

<<>>

The ***George***, a 200-foot wooden schooner, was loaded with 1,330 tons of coal when she ran into a gale-driven snowstorm on October 24, 1893. She lies in 15 feet of water at the mouth of a cove near Mosquito Beach. The crew survived by rowing a yawl ashore.

<<>>

The ***Herman H. Hettler***, a 210-foot wooden steamer, sank after piling up on the Trout Point reef during a November 23, 1926, snowstorm. A cargo of 1,100 tons of edible salt was lost. A few years after the *Hettler* went down, her remains were dynamited because they were a navigational hazard.

<<>>

The ***Kiowa***, a 251-foot steel bulk freight steamer, was hit by a gale force storm in November 1929. The grain-carrying vessel is found at 20-40-foot depths. On clear days, huge sections of her hull are visible from the surface.

<<>>

The ***Manhattan***, a 252-foot wooden-hulled freighter, sank October 26, 1903, after a cabin fire. The *Manhattan* burned to the waterline.

<<>>

The ***Mary M. Scott***, a 100-foot canal schooner loaded with iron ore, was driven ashore on November 2, 1870. The wreck rests in about 15 feet of water 500 feet off the Sand Point channel buoy.

<<>>

The ***Michael Groh***, a steam barge, sank a mile northeast of Sand Point and three miles west of Miners Castle on November 22, 1895. She carried 325,000 board feet of lumber to the bottom with her.

<<>>

The ***Smith Moore***, a 260-foot three-masted wooden steamer, collided with the ***James Pickands*** as the *Pickands* was being towed by the ***M.M. Drake*** on July 13, 1889. As a result of the collision the *Smith Moore* sank. She is the best known and most dramatic wreck in the preserve because hers are the most intact remains of any wreck in the area.

<<>>

The ***Steven M. Selvick***, a 71-foot steel tug, was intentionally sunk. Selvick Marine Towing Company was looking to scrap the vessel. Foresighted individuals had the idea that she would make a great shipwreck dive site and wildlife habitat. In May 1996, the intact ship was sunk off Trout Point. Only 20 feet below the surface, she is a perfect dive for beginners.

<<>>

The ***Superior***, a 191 foot, two-deck side-wheel steamer, is the most tragic of the Pictured Rocks accidents. On October 28, 1856, the *Superior,* whose upper deck was reserved for passengers, lost her course. Heavy seas threatened to bring her down. The crew attempted to throw the cargo overboard to lighten the load, but the ill-fated ship took on water which put out the boiler fires. She foundered on the rocks, and passengers were plunged overboard. Many were able to swim through the frigid waters to the rocks and clung there until they were rescued. Between 35 and 42 of those aboard died in the wreck.

<<>>

The ***Wabash***, a schooner being towed by the *Samson*, a consort, tried to reach safety on Grand Island during a raging November 15, 1883, snowstorm. The snowstorm won, and the *Wabash* ran aground. Fortunately, the *Wabash* crew was taken aboard the *Samson*. There was no loss of lives. Broken and scattered with her cargo, the *Wabash* was a total loss.

• The Famous or Infamous with Ties to Munising

Connie Binsfeld, 58th Lieutenant Governor of Michigan, was born in Munising in 1924 and attended area schools. She was an advocate for the environment and the rights of women and children.

<<>>

George Snow Hill, a muralist painter and sculptor, was born in Munising in 1898. He studied abroad, met and married another artist, Polly Knipp, before returning to the U.S. He established a studio in St. Petersburg, Florida, but courted controversy for his racist murals.

<<>>

Steven J. Raica, Roman Catholic priest, fifth Bishop of Gaylord, Michigan, and fifth Bishop of Birmingham, Alabama, was born in Munising.

<<>>

Brock Strom, professional football player, was born in Munising. He became the U.S. Air Force Academy's first All-American. Strom played tackle on the offensive and defensive lines at a time when it wasn't unusual for players to have positions on both offense and defense.

• Books and Movies with Ties to Munising

Robert Ritchie, better known as **Kid Rock**, a Detroit-based musician, filmed a portion of his video, ***Born Free***, during a visit to the Pictured Rocks National Lakeshore.

<<>>

Death at the Lighthouse, Loren Graham, (2013). (See Ghost Story.) This is how the book is described on Amazon:

In 1972 Loren Graham and his wife purchased the Old North Lighthouse on Grand Island near Pictured Rocks National Lakeshore. The lighthouse was built in 1867 and stands on a 200-foot rock cliff on the northwest side of the island in Lake Superior. Inside the cracked and crumbling yellow brick walls of the lighthouse, under the oilcloth on the kitchen table, Graham discovered a yellowing newspaper clipping from the *Detroit Free Press* from June 15, 1908. It read, "Grand Island Lighthouse keeper and his assistant believed to be victims of brutal murder and robbery." What happened to the 1908 lighthouse keeper and his assistant? Graham set out to answer this question. *Death at the Lighthouse* is the summary of Graham's thirty years of research which includes an analysis of the factors of this unsolved mystery in Michigan's Upper Peninsula.

• GHOST STORY

The Ghost of the Grand Island North Lighthouse. On June 14, 1908, a special supplement to the *New York Times* carried details of a brutal homicide on Grand Island just off the shore of Munising. More than a century later, the killing remains a cold case. The answers to the mutilation and murder of assistant lighthouse keeper Edward Morrison will likely never be known, but there are some pretty good hunches. What happened to George Genery, the main lighthouse keeper, is also fodder for speculation. The best guess is he committed the murder.

A month before he died, 30-year-old Morrison, who by all accounts was a cheerful, good-natured man, left his home in Flint, Michigan, and traveled north. He and his wife struggled financially, and he was eager to begin his job as the assistant keeper at Grand Island Lighthouse. He had heard rumors that George Genery, the keeper at the lighthouse, was a tough taskmaster as well as being a humorless man with a violent temper. No assistant keeper had lasted more than one season working with Genery.

Morrison was unconcerned. This was the career opportunity he had dreamed of, and he felt certain he could soften the heart of the crusty keeper. He believed that as constant companions to each other, they'd become friends. Edward kissed his wife of two years goodbye and promised his first order of business in the north country would be finding them a house and calling for her to join him. They would then enjoy a long-delayed honeymoon.

That isn't the way things worked out. In early June, days before his death, Morrison sent a letter to family indicating that "If you should find my body along the shores of Lake Superior, you will know I have had some difficulty." The young assistant keeper described his boss in an ugly mood and drinking excessively. Not long after, the townspeople noticed the lighthouse had gone dark. Its beacon wasn't seen for several days.

On June 12, 1908, six weeks after Morrison had arrived in the area, his body was found in a small sailboat that belonged to the lighthouse. It had washed ashore near Au Sable Point. The body was battered and maimed beyond recognition. It appeared the corpse had been beaten mercilessly about the head and shoulders with a club, leaving remains that didn't look human. Identification wasn't immediately possible. However, locals were familiar with a distinctive 13-star tattoo on the deceased's left arm, and confirmed his death by that inked marking.

In an interesting aside to the case, the first coroner's jury concluded the death was due to exposure to the rough weather the area had suffered five days earlier. The conclusion was so preposterous that a second coroner's jury was asked to examine the body. This jury concluded that "while they were not able to tell how he died," they had a strong suspicion it was murder.

The reasonable next step involved sending investigators to talk to keeper, George Genery. Upon arrival at the lighthouse, they found supplies that Genery had transported from Munising piled on the dock—an empty wheelbarrow for getting them to the lighthouse was nearby. Genery's coat hung, undisturbed on a hook in the boathouse, his vest was draped over the back of a chair, his watch and carefully folded papers were in the pocket.

The final entry in the log was made on June 5, but it gave no clue about what might have gone wrong. Nothing else seemed out of order at the lighthouse. Except that there was no sign of George Genery, and continued searches never revealed his whereabouts.

Three boats belonged to the lighthouse, and the investigators quibbled over whether only one was missing (the one containing Morrison's body) or whether a second boat was also missing.

Many locals claimed to have seen Genery between June 9 and 12 when Morrison's body was discovered. They described the keeper as drinking heavily. Investigators met with Genery's wife who lived in Munising. She insisted she had no idea of her husband's current whereabouts, and she seemed curiously unconcerned by his disappearance.

Several theories were proposed, none given official sanction. The first explanation was the least malevolent. It supposed that the keeper and his assistant went out to lift their fishing nets, and that the keeper fell overboard and drowned. The assistant keeper, this theory further speculates, didn't know how to handle the sailboat and drifted until he died from exposure. This explanation seems easy to discredit. Morrison's family insisted Edward was an expert sailor and had owned a 32-foot sailboat that he captained on the Detroit River. Further, this story didn't account for the mutilated body.

The next hypothesis suggested that the two men received their wages on June 6, and that someone, knowing they were flush with money, robbed, killed, and dumped their bodies into the sailboats and set them adrift.

Supposedly a second body was discovered sometime later in the east channel, but it was so badly decomposed that it was never identified. Interestingly, this theory must be the support for a memorial posted claiming that George Genery died in 1908 and is buried in Alger County's Maple Grove Cemetery near Munising. Whether the body discovered was Genery has not been conclusively established.

The third, and a reasonable explanation for Morrison's death, is that Genery and Morrison argued, Genery murdered his assistant keeper, and then Genery disappeared. This theory seems consistent with Genery's temper, the letter Morrison sent to his family indicating he feared for his life, and the condition of Morrison's body when found. However, if offers no explanation for why there was no evidence of the crime at the lighthouse, nor why George was never seen again. (For additional detail, see Books and Movies with Ties to Munising.)

After the murder, additional keepers have served at the Grand Island North Lighthouse, and there have been reports of whistling from someone walking the shore. Often all that can be seen are wisps of smoke. However, other reports describe a man holding up his left arm to reveal thirteen stars.

12. Marquette

USA Today's Readers' Choice Awards proclaimed Marquette the top small town for adventure in the U.S. *CBS MoneyWatch* called Marquette one of the ten best places to retire in the country (You better like lots and lots and lots of snow). It is a town colored by delicious contrasts. Shakespeare performed in a brewery. Listening to jazz while taking in the grandeur of Superior. Audacious hiking and snowmobile trails, but also art galleries and cultural events. Blue jeans and red flannel shirts paired with a stormy kromer or boutique ensembles. A pasty (pass tee) with gravy or organic, vegetarian, vegan, and gluten-free, whatever you are hankering for, you can accommodate your taste buds. Expect the unexpected and know that whatever you seek, you should find that and more in Marquette.

Marquette, the largest city in da Yoop, is still a small town. The 2020 population was 20,866. Visited by missionaries and fur traders in the 1600s and 1700s, real development began in the mid-1800s when iron deposits were discovered in the area. Jackson Mining Company was organized in 1845. In 1849 the Marquette Iron Company formed, and in the wake of its founding, the small village of Marquette was established. First called New Worcester, the name was changed in 1850 to honor the Jesuit missionary, Father Jacques Marquette. The Marquette Iron Company foundered and failed, but its successor, the Cleveland Iron Mining Company organized and flourished.

All the mining activity was linked by railroad, and Marquette became the hub and leading shipping center in the Upper Peninsula. The town prospered, and alongside its advantageous mining activity, Marquette developed as a summer tourist haven.

Several small islands including Middle Island, Gull Island, Lover's Island, Presque Isle Point Rocks, White Rocks, Ripley Rock, and Picnic Rocks lie in Lake Superior and are part of the city. The Marquette Underwater Preserve, immediately offshore, garners the attention of divers interested in exploring ships resting there.

You won't lack activities in Marquette. Fishing in the cold, deep lake rewards you with a delicious dinner—a catch of lake trout, whitefish, or salmon. Bikers, hikers, and walkers use the extensive network of paths and cross-country ski trails. Especially favored are those at Presque Isle Park and the Fit Strip.

Northern Michigan University offers the community educational and cultural activities. The Forest Roberts Theatre is one of the finest university theaters in the nation, and it presents live stage productions and dance ensembles. The university's Black Box Theatre is a smaller and more intimate venue with a 100-seat capacity for its many student productions. The Kaufman Auditorium, part of the Graveraet School, is home to theatre productions, classes, and lectures. Graveraet and Lake Superior Theatre offer summer stock. If you are in Marquette with a bit of extra time, check the university website to see what is happening.

• Museums

Beaumier Heritage Center, in Gries Hall 7th Street and Lee Drive. This historical museum is located on the campus of Northern Michigan University. Its mission is the promotion and preservation of the Upper Peninsula's past through exhibitions and educational public programs. The center collects and displays artifacts related to the history of Northern Michigan University.

<<>>

DeVos Art Museum, 1401 Presque Isle Avenue, a regional art museum for the Upper Peninsula, is located on the campus of Northern Michigan University. It houses over 1,500 objects in its permanent collection and features exhibits of local, regional, and international art.

<<>>

Marquette Art and Culture Center, 217 North Front Street, in the Peter White Public Library. The center supports visual, cultural, and creative arts through education, exhibition, performance, and community projects. If you are in Marquette, you can see what is currently happening at the center.

<<>>

Marquette Children's Museum, 123 West Baraga Avenue, is a perfect place for kids to explore and give free rein to their imaginations. The staff allows children (under supervision) to observe, pet, and touch small lizards and turtles outside their cages. In the Fantastic Forest, little ones can sit in a kid-sized bird nest perched in a giant tree. Or they can explore stores lining a child-sized street. The museum offers a playroom and an educational playground, both meant to encourage kids to be kids.

<<>>

The **Marquette Maritime Museum**, 300 North Lakeshore Boulevard. The museum features an exhibit and story of the *Edmund Fitzgerald* whose last radioed words were, "We are holding our own."

Marquette Maritime Museum. Courtesy of Bob Royce.

The wreck of the *Henry B. Smith* comes to life in another exhibit. The *Smith* went down in the historic Storm of 1913 taking her crew of 25 to their deaths. The remains of the *Smith* stayed hidden until a century later, when in May 2013 she was found 500 feet below the surface of Lake Superior, 30 miles out from Marquette.

The McClintock Annex to the Maritime Museum features a large three-dimensional diorama depicting the Battle of Leyte Gulf in the Philippines, October 23-26, 1944, arguably the largest naval battle in history (depending on the criteria used in defining what constitutes a battle). The museum has a large collection of WWII submarine memorabilia.

The Museum maintains the **Marquette Harbor Lighthouse**, 300 N. Lakeshore, an active aid to current navigation. One-hour tours are given, but reservations are requested.

Funds for the lighthouse were approved in 1850 to help ships navigate to the ore docks, the light was constructed in 1852, and the first beam illuminated the water in 1853. By 1865 the lighthouse had suffered serious deterioration and additional funds were appropriated for a replacement tower. In 1875 a breakwater was constructed to minimize the forces of wind and waves on the lighthouse. In spite of the breakwater, a major storm destroyed the light in 1889, and a new light was constructed on a crib at the southernmost end of the breakwater. That same year, the lighthouse was electrified. In 2002 a thirty-year lease was signed by the Marquette Maritime Museum, which became responsible for the maintenance and control of the lighthouse.

<<>>

The **Marquette Regional History Center**, 145 West Spring Street, provides a history of the area from 10,000 years ago to the present. Signage and displays educate visitors about Michigan's Upper Peninsula with exhibits describing the first people, Native American Culture, the fur trade era, agriculture, logging, mining, and other aspects of U.P. life. You might also be interested in the Center's walking tours of the area.

• Beaches, Parks, and Trails

Presque Isle Park, on the north side of Marquette, is 323 acres of mostly forested land that juts into Lake Superior. The name means “almost an island,” and the French must have felt that the narrow strip of land that connects Presque Isle to Marquette prevented it from being a true island. Locals often ignore the “almost” and refer to it as the island. Whatever you call it, the views, added to amenities that include picnic tables, barbecue pits, playground, a band shell for concerts, a pavilion, a gazebo, a marina, a concession stand, walking, and cross-country skiing trails, and Moosewood Nature Center, create a park favored by locals and visitors alike.

The **Black Rocks** are a short hike from the tip of the park. They are known as the place to jump off the cliff into Lake Superior. If that seems a bit drastic, you can simply sit and appreciate the views.

While at Presque Isle Park, check out the **Upper Harbor Iron Ore Dock**, also called the Presque Isle Dock. Built in 1911, the dock is still in use, and approximately ten million tons of ore are shipped from there each year. The steel-framed structure is 1,250 feet long and 60 feet wide. The top deck sits 75 feet above water level. The dock is supported by 10,000 wooden piles.

Ore is brought to the dock by railcar and dumped into 200 steel pockets or bins with a storage capacity of 50,000 tons.

Boats are loaded by lowering a chute to an open cargo hatch aboard the vessel. (See Lower Harbor Ore Docks under Other Things to See or Do.)

<<>>

Sugarloaf Mountain presents the opportunity for a perfect hike. Sugarloaf offers two trails, one marked “easy” which is slightly longer but has a more even grade, and a rockier, more difficult trail with a greater number of stairs. There are benches along the way, and either trail will take you to a stunning vista 470 feet above Lake Superior.

<<>>

South Beach Park, on the south side of Marquette, is a long, wide stretch of sand that is both family and pet-friendly. A patch of beach is reserved for dogs to frolic free of restraint. Amenities: calm, shallow swimming spot that's good for children, restrooms, playground, and parking.

<<>>

McCarty's Cove, flanked by the red U.S. Coast Guard Station Lighthouse on its south shore, offers a reprieve from hot summer days. Amenities include picnic areas, grills, playground, restrooms, and lifeguard during swimming season.

<<>>

Other Parks. On weekends, if you want a less crowded park, there are plenty to consider. Local maps will show you how to find them and describe amenities for Tourist Park (with camping facilities), Founder's Landing, LaBonte Park, Mattson Lower Harbor Park, Park Cemetery, Shiras Park, Williams Park, Harlow Park, Pocket Park, Spring Street Park, and Father Marquette Park.

<<>>

Dead River Falls, slightly west of Marquette, has a number of dams and diversions that run wild for a half-mile. There are three significant falls and several lesser drops. This may be the best waterfall adventure of your trip, but it isn't an easy trail. Wear good shoes, spray yourself with mosquito repellent, and dress for the weather.

• Other Stops to Consider

Lower Harbor Ore Docks. The Lower Harbor Ore Docks are remnants of Marquette's past. At one time, multiple ore docks serviced the harbor, and there are plans to revitalize and repurpose these striking icons that grace the downtown Marquette waterfront.

Lower Harbor Ore Docks.
Courtesy of Pixabay Free Images.

<<>>

Northern Michigan University is worth a stop before leaving town. NMU is home to the Wildcats and has one of the prettiest campuses in the nation. It is the location of several small museums. (See Museums.)

• LIGHTHOUSES

(See Marquette Harbor Lighthouse under Museums.)

<<>>

The Presque Isle Harbor Breakwater Light stands on the breakwater at the northeast side of Presque Isle Harbor in Marquette. In 2016 it was added to the National Register of Historic Places in Michigan. The lighthouse is 55 feet tall with a rectangular concrete pier at the base, an octagonal concrete first story, and a three-story steel light tower. The white tower has a red band at its midsection. The tower is accessed by a ladder through the ceiling of the lower level. The lighthouse has three rooms and a closet. The lighthouse is an important aid to navigation and can be seen from Presque Isle Park. For a closer view of the lighthouse and views of incoming freighters, you can walk out on the breakwater when weather permits.

<<>>

Stannard Rock Lighthouse is close to "nowhere." Yes, that's how one travel writer explained its location. It is 40 miles north of Marquette's shore and can only be seen by air or boat. Locals describe it as the loneliest place on the planet. The lighthouse was named for Charles Stannard who first discovered the dangerous one-mile reef off the coast of Marquette. Construction brought problems of nightmare proportions; the project extended over five years, and the light first beamed its warning signal in 1883. The lighthouse is under the control of the United States Coast Guard. It was automated in 1962 and remains active. The lighthouse is not open to the public, and braving dangerous waters for a closer view is unwise. The best advice if you want to see it is to buy a picture but otherwise don't try to get too close.

• SHIPWRECKS

The Marquette Underwater Preserve has several wrecks of interest.

The ***Charles J. Kershaw***, a wooden steamer, foundered in a storm on September 29, 1895. The *Kershaw* was towing two schooner barges when she lost power. Her crew was rescued by the men of the Marquette Lifesaving Station. Pieces of the *Kershaw* lie scattered and broken in about 25 feet of water. Her substantial boiler is a dive highlight.

<<>>

The ***D. Leuty*** was lost on October 31, 1911, while she struggled to enter Marquette Harbor with her cargo of logs. The *Leuty* came to rest near downtown Marquette about 800 feet off Lighthouse Point. The ship was broken up, and her engine, boiler, and machinery were salvaged. Three substantial parts of the hull and her large rudder remain in about 40 feet of water.

<<>>

The ***DeSoto*** was launched April 10, 1856, and broke up on December 4, 1869. Her framing and planking are in about ten feet of water and make an easy novice dive or snorkeling opportunity.

<<>>

The ***Florida***, a two-masted schooner, smashed against the Marquette docks during a blizzard on November 17, 1886. One crewman lost his life. The ship's remains rest in shallow water covered by shifting sand.

<<>>

In addition to shipwrecks, the Marquette Underwater Preserve has many docks and cribs and unusual geology for divers to explore.

• The Famous or Infamous with Ties to Marquette

Michael Todd Bordick was born in Marquette on July 21, 1965. He played Major League Baseball from 1990-2003.

<<>>

Alfred Shaddock Burt, an American jazz musician, is best known for the 15 Christmas Carols he wrote. Burt was born in Marquette. Only one of his Christmas Carols was sung publicly before his death, but after death he achieved fame. "Caroling, Caroling" and "Some Children See Him" are his most recorded carols. Simon and Garfunkel recorded his "The Star Carol." His carols have been sung by Andy Williams, Kenny Loggins, James Taylor, and George Winston.

<<>>

Anthony Chebatoris holds the dubious honor of being the only person executed in the State of Michigan since the state, in 1846, became the first English speaking government in the world to ban capital punishment.

In 1928 Chebatoris was imprisoned at Marquette for armed robbery. After his release, he continued his life of crime, and on September 29, 1937, he and an accomplice attempted to rob a Midland, Michigan, bank. In the course of committing that felony, the crooks shot two bank employees, both of whom survived. The robbers, upset about how the crime was unraveling, abandoned their scheme and fled. However, a dentist in the building adjacent to the bank had heard the gunshots, and as the robbers drove away, he fired his hunting rifle at the getaway car from his second-story office window.

Chebatoris was struck. The wounded man and his partner jumped from their car to search for the shooter. A truck driver with horrible timing happened to be passing. The driver had the further misfortune to be wearing a cap and uniform mistaken by the robbers as a police uniform. The two criminals shot and killed the poor fellow. The dentist then fatally shot Chebatoris' partner. Chebatoris fled on foot but was soon captured.

He was charged with the crime under the Federal Bank Robbery Act of 1934 that made bank robbery and its related crimes a federal offense. Chebatoris' trial was held in federal court in Bay City. The jury had the option of imposing a death sentence and did so. Governor Frank Murphy tried to get the sentence commuted to life in prison, but the federal government wouldn't agree to a commutation. (See The Famous and the Infamous with Ties to Harbor Beach in Book One, *Exploring Michigan's Sunrise Coasts.*) Murphy then requested that the execution be moved to another state—a request he took to President Franklin Roosevelt—and that request was likewise denied.

On July 8, 1938, Chebatoris was hanged on a Federal Prison Farm outside Milan, Michigan. He was the only convict executed in the state in the past 175 years.

<<>>

Susan Vanita Diol, an American actress, who played supporting roles in more than 40 television series, was born on May 25, 1962, in Marquette. Diol had roles in *Night Court, Seinfeld, One Life to Live, Star Trek-The Next*

Generation, *Star Trek-Voyager*, *NCIS*, *CSI*, *Quantum Leap*, and *Wings*. Diol married four times. Her second marriage was to actor and singer Shaun Cassidy.

<<>>

Dallas Drake, a former professional ice hockey winger with the National Hockey League, played college hockey at Northern Michigan University in Marquette where he was a key player in the team's winning 1991 season. Drafted by the Detroit Red Wings in the sixth round of the early NHL draft in 1989, Drake also played for the Winnipeg Jets, the Phoenix Coyotes, and the St. Louis Blues.

<<>>

Nita Engle, an American watercolorist, was an art director and magazine illustrator. She attended high school in Marquette and studied at Northern Michigan University. She set up a studio overlooking the waters of Lake Superior. She exhibited her work in the United States and abroad. She received an honorary doctorate from Northern Michigan University. *American Artist Magazine* named her "Artist of the Year" in 1984. Her life was the subject of a documentary, *Wilderness Palette—Nita Engle in Michigan*. She authored a book, *Make a Watercolor Paint Itself: Experimental Techniques for Achieving Realistic Effects*. Engle died on August 29, 2019, in Ishpeming.

<<>>

Robert Erickson, an American Composer, was born in 1917 in Marquette. Erickson taught at the College of St. Catherine in St. Paul, Minnesota, San Francisco State College, and the University of California at Berkeley. With composer Wilbur Ogdon, he founded the music department at the University of California, San Diego. He received a Guggenheim Fellowship, a Ford Foundation Fellowship, and was elected a Fellow of the Institute for Creative Arts at the University of California. His string quartet, Solstice, won the 1985 Friedham Award for Chamber Music. Two books have been written about Erickson's life and music:

Thinking Sound Music: The Life and Work of Robert Erickson (Charles Shere), and *Music of Many Means: Sketches and Essays on the Music of Robert Erickson* (Robert Erickson and John MacKay).

<<>>

Justin Florek was born on May 18, 1990, in Marquette. He was selected by the Boston Bruins in the fifth round of the 2010 NHL Entry Draft. He played professional hockey with the South Carolina Stingrays. Prior to his professional career, Florek played 157 games for the Northern Michigan University Wildcats at Marquette. During those games, he scored 53 goals and was credited with 63 assists for 116 points.

<<>>

Vernon Forrest was the first member of his family to graduate from high school. His family had moved from Augusta, Georgia, to Marquette where he attended and graduated from Marquette Senior High School. He attended Northern Michigan University on a scholarship. He was a member of the 1992 U.S. Summer Olympic Team in Barcelona, Spain, but had his dreams sabotaged by food poisoning. In spite of that disappointment, he went on to box professionally from 1992 through 2008 when he met with the ultimate tragedy. Forrest pulled into a gas station in Atlanta, Georgia, and was putting air into a tire when he was robbed at gunpoint. His assailant fled. Forrest, who was armed, gave chase. He abandoned his pursuit after a couple of blocks. He stopped and talked to a second man who, unbeknownst to Forrest, was part of the robbery. This second man shot Forrest in the back seven times. Forrest died at the scene. He was 38 years old. He is remembered not only for his boxing feats but for his charity work.

<<>>

Jimmy Peters Sr., known as Shakey Peters played professional ice hockey for the Detroit Red Wings and won

Stanley Cups in 1950 and 1954. He died on October 11, 2006, at age 84, in Marquette.

<<>>

Hjalmar Peterson was a Marquette comedian who during the 1940s found a niche as a Scandinavian Vaudeville act. He performed in the persona of Olle i Skratthult. He owned a popular bar and dance hall in Marquette, but while performing, he spoke only Swedish. When second-generation Scandinavian immigrants began speaking English, his audience dwindled. He ended his career as a gospel singer.

<<>>

Matthew Songer invented the Songer Cable used in spinal surgery. He is a surgeon and the former chairman of the board of Pioneer Surgical Technology, a corporation he founded in Marquette in 1992. Songer and the Songer Cable were featured in the book, *Contemporary Management of Spinal Cord Injuries: From Impact to Rehabilitation.*

<<>>

John D. Voelker practiced law in Marquette and wrote *Anatomy of a Murder.* (See Books and Movies with Ties to Marquette.)

<<>>

Peter White was a founding father of Marquette. Born in 1830, he had his hand in banking, business, real estate development including iron mining, and eventually went to law school. He was a director of the Cleveland Iron Company. He held many public offices including state representative and senator. In his later years, he was recognized for his philanthropy.

In 1849 Robert J. Graveraet had arrived on Mackinac Island seeking men to accompany him to the newly discovered iron fields of the Upper Peninsula. White joined the adventure, although it meant a pay cut. The men headed across the U.P. and claimed land west of Jackson

Mine near what is now Ishpeming. More men arrived on a second ship, and the workers cleared land and erected buildings in Marquette to house a machine shop, forge, and a sawmill. Graveraet established the Marquette Iron Company in 1849, and four years later the company closed. The Cleveland Company purchased the assets of Marquette, including the company store where Peter White worked. White continued his company store, but as an employee of the Cleveland Company.

• Books and Movies with Ties to Marquette

Anatomy of a Murder, a courtroom drama, was written in 1958 by Robert Traver. The book's background is nearly as interesting as the wildly successful book itself. Robert Traver was the pen name of John D. Voelker who was born in Ishpeming, Michigan, attended the University of Michigan Law School, practiced law in Marquette, and was the Prosecuting Attorney of Marquette County from 1935 to 1950. From 1956 to 1960, he served as a Michigan Supreme Court Justice appointed by Governor G. Mennen Williams. Voelker didn't think it seemed appropriate for a sitting Supreme Court Justice to write novels on government time, so he adopted the pen name Robert Traver, Robert for his dead brother's first name, and Traver which was his mother's maiden name. As Robert Traver, he wrote ten books including *Laughing Whitefish* which was also set in Marquette. Voelker was an avid fisherman his entire life and wrote several tomes on fishing.

Anatomy of a Murder was made into a movie directed by Otto Preminger. It starred an A-list cast including Eve Arden, Ben Gazzara, George C. Scott, Jimmy Stewart, Lee Remick, and Orson Bean. The film was nominated for seven academy awards (it won none). The story was based on a 1952 case in which Voelker was the defense attorney. In the book and film version, the lawyer is a folksy local attorney. In the movie, the attorney is played by Jimmy

Stewart. The defendant is Manny Manion (Gazzara), a U.S. Army Lieutenant who is charged with murdering bartender Barney Quill. Manion claims he has no direct memory of the murder itself, but claims Quill raped his wife (Lee Remick) whose reputation as a loose woman is put on trial.

Marquette County Courthouse. Courtesy of Pixabay Free Images.

Manion's defense isn't that he was innocent of the charges, but that his actions were the result of an irresistible impulse. Much of the movie was filmed in the Marquette County Courthouse and the neighboring environs of Marquette and Big Bay County. Later in his life, Voelker earned more royalties from his book than he earned in salary from his legal endeavors.

<<>>

Indian Country, written by Philip Caputo author of several novels about the war in Vietnam, is set in Michigan's Upper Peninsula with many scenes depicting Marquette. Protagonist Christian Starkmann and his boyhood friend, an Ojibwe Native American named Bonny George, head from the wilderness of Michigan's U.P. to Vietnam where George is killed. Starkmann returns home to northern Michigan but is haunted by memories of combat and the loss of the childhood friend with whom he hunted and fished. Starkmann suffers hallucinations, and the ghost of George forces him to confront a secret Starkmann has kept buried. If exposed, that secret could destroy everything Starkmann holds dear.

<<>>

True North is Jim Harrison's novel about a Marquette family that grew wealthy exploiting the Upper Peninsula's timber. David Burkett faces the legacy handed down to him by his father's sins and his mother's alcoholism and pill addiction. He and his sister are left mainly to raise themselves. Family tragedy is layered on betrayal and a need to make things right again.

<<>>

Middlesex, written by Jeffrey Eugenides, won the 2003 Pulitzer Prize for Fiction, and Eugenides was hailed one of the best young authors by *New Yorker Magazine*. In 1974 Calliope Stephanides, a student at a girls' school in Grosse Pointe, finds herself drawn to a classmate with a gift for acting. A relationship develops between the two young students. Callie's desires and her failure to develop like other girls convince her she is not really a girl. The explanation for this situation takes the reader back to a village where two lovers and one rare mutation cause a metamorphosis that makes Callie both mythical and real. The book spans eight decades and explores the complicities of gender and desire. Eugenides refers to Marquette by name, in addition to other locations in Michigan.

<<>>

Blankets is the story of a young man coming of age and finding the confidence to express his creative voice. Written by Craig Thompson, it is a graphic memoir of an adolescent growing up in a fundamentalist Christian home. Craig and Raina fall in love at winter church camp. They share their angst and struggles with religion, revealing to one another their dreams of escape. The novel, the winner of two Eisner and three Harvey Awards, captures adolescent yearning, first love (and first heartache), crisis, and healing. Beautifully rendered in pen and ink, Thompson has created a lasting love story. Much of the book takes place in Marquette.

<<>>

The ***Adult Swim*** television series, *Joe Pera Talks with You*, was partially filmed in and around the city of Marquette. The series stars a fictionalized version of comedian Joe Pera as a choir teacher living in Marquette, talking directly to his audience about mundane topics like iron, Sunday breakfast, fall drives, and sleeping.

• Ghost Stories

Ghosts of Holy Cross Orphanage (aka Old City Orphanage). Many stories lurk in the recesses of this historic building. Two seem more prevalent than others. The tragic history of the building—its purpose, the abuses, and the neglect—are as notable as the ghost stories. Let's start with the ghost stories.

Helka[1] was brought to the orphanage by her father who couldn't care for her. He was a fisherman who spent his days on the water working to earn enough money to survive. His wife had died from typhoid. Little Helka understood none of this. She believed no one cared about her. Her father's promise to come back for her seemed as empty as her life loomed devoid of joy. The nuns, some kind and sweet, others not so much, didn't dispense love and affection as generously as they meted out religion and rules and punishment. The Sister that Helka called Atilla the Nun was a master of the twisted ear, the pinched

Old City Orphanage.
Courtesy of Pixabay Free Images.

[1] Names are fictitious.

collar bone, the threat of no supper, or worse—the threat of God's damnation.

Helka sat on the built-in seat of the multi-paned window, one leg tucked under her and the other dangling about six inches from the floor. She was a scrawny child for her seven years, whether a result of genetics or her loss of appetite and meager portions of food served by the severe-faced French nuns, wasn't an issue that concerned anyone. Helka was the youngest of the twenty-four girls who shared the dormitory-style room with its three sets of bunk beds neatly lined up and perfectly made on each of the two long side walls. Starting in 1915, when it opened, and for fifty years thereafter, as many as 200 children at a time called the Old City Orphanage their home. During that half century, many urban legends took root.

Helka turned her head and fingered the chintz curtains pulled back to reveal a dull gray world beyond the walls that imprisoned her. She stared at the city of Marquette and wondered if it offered any hope of happiness for her when she was old enough to find her own way. Then something akin to a miracle happened. The sun peeked out from behind the clouds in the winter sky, and snowflakes began drifting, large and lazy, to the ground. Helka grabbed her coat and galoshes and looked down the hall for any nun who might obstruct her path to the stairs and the outside door. There was no one.

At first the afternoon promised a reprieve. She had risen, like every other day, at 6:00 a.m. Mornings were set aside for early worship, classes, and study. But for a short time before dinner, her hours were her own. She was expected to review her lessons, help the nuns with cleaning tasks, and otherwise serve God. On this particular afternoon, she decided to steal some time for herself. She closed the heavy front door behind her and beelined for the treed ridge at the property's edge. She sat on a log and watched a squirrel jump from branch to branch above her.

In a heartbeat, she would have traded places with the bushy-tailed rodent.

As the sun started slipping low, the chill in the air sent Helka back to the orphanage. Her boots leaked and her feet were wet and stinging cold. She hadn't taken time for a scarf or a sweater under her thin winter coat. The orphanage looked a long way off in the distance.

When she climbed the front steps, her teeth chattered and her fingers were numb. She tried to open the door, but it was locked. She pounded, but no one came. Maybe everyone was at dinner. She continued banging, and tears rolled down her cheeks. When Sister Atilla finally opened the door, Helka was suffering hypothermia, although no one back then called it that. She was told to put on her nightclothes and crawl under the covers of her bed to get warm. No one offered her dinner or seemed concerned with her plight other than to scold her for leaving without telling anyone.

The next morning Helka ached all over. She sneezed, coughed, and gripped a handkerchief to stanch her runny nose. By the time a doctor was called, she had pneumonia. A few days later she died.

Not to miss an opportunity to make a disciplinary point, the nuns displayed the child's body in the basement and held a private service for the orphans to see firsthand what happened to little boys and girls who misbehaved. Many of the children had nightmares for weeks. Small wonder that Helka haunts the orphanage.

The second ghost haunting the Old City Orphanage is a young boy, maybe a year or so one way or the other from Helka's age. He stuttered and looked at the world through the rheumy eyes of an old man. One nun believed this child was deserving of the Maker's displeasure. She made the boy's life unbearable. One night after everyone else had gone to sleep, the lad took his sheets, twisted them into a rope, and hung himself. The cause of his death was listed as accidental, but he had never forgotten the treatment he had endured. After death his spirit, like Helka's, remained to haunt the old orphanage.

It is said that when everything else is quiet, neighbors still hear children sobbing from somewhere within the orphanage walls.

Ghost stories cannot be proven or disproven. Many of those connected to the orphanage refute the allegations of misconduct. Still, the rumors persist.

What is the real story of the orphanage? Marquette seems to have had an unusual dedication to its orphanages. Whether that interest was human compassion or something else can be argued. Marquette's first orphanage was built in the 1870s and called The Rock. In 1881 The Rock was followed by a Catholic orphanage named St. Joseph in Assinins. Within two decades, both orphanages were overcrowded, and Bishop Frederick Eis began soliciting funds for a new, bigger orphanage—an orphanage intended to be the biggest in the Upper Peninsula. Since the U.P. was sparsely populated, the need for housing so many orphans seemed disproportional. The first orphanages were opened only to white children. Parents who died of disease or accident often left the state the burden of housing and raising their children. Sad, that there were no aunts or uncles or grandparents to step up, not even foster or adoptive parents for an unwanted child. Then something more sinister, especially with the advantage of hindsight, crept into society's thinking. The government instituted a policy that turned the orphanages from white-only to a place to house Native American children who were taken from their parents to teach them to accept and assimilate into white culture. The stories from Native children who were housed in the facilities are chilling, an indictment of a lack of respect for their culture or the needs of a child for a nurturing family.

The 1960s brought about a change in attitudes, and the last children to live in the old city orphanage were Cuban refugees who fled or were transported from their homeland in search of sanctuary. Many of them were placed with adoptive parents. By the late 1960s, the last orphan had left. For years, the building served as offices. By 1982 the building with a historic façade, architectural appeal, and an often-grim history was deserted. It fell into disrepair and became an eyesore—an attractive nuisance to curiosity seekers who trespassed onto its premises. Late at night under the cloak of darkness, interlopers poked around the private property. They peeked through broken windows at trash-littered floors and crumbling walls. Some claimed they were welcomed by a teary-eyed old man who had lived there as a child.

There were calls for tearing down the blighted building. Other citizens rallied in support of repurposing the structure and maintaining the historic importance. More years passed without a clear path for what was to become of the property. A purchaser acquired the building with the hope of turning it into an assisted living facility. That goal never materialized. Ultimately, in 1997 a group of developers gutted and renovated the interior, cleaned up the overgrown trees and shrubbery outside, and opened the building as Grandview Marquette with 56 low-income housing units. The building is currently on the Michigan List of Historic Places. Maybe at long last, the majestic building has found a noble purpose. And maybe the ghosts of all of the children who suffered there are finally at rest.

<<>>

The Haunted Landmark Inn, like the Old Catholic Orphanage above, is recognized for its architectural beauty and historic significance. And like the Orphanage, the Inn is said to be haunted.

Investors first became interested in building the hotel in 1910. The location, high enough for a bird's-eye look at the city, promised spectacular views of Lake Superior. Years passed before the ambitious plans reached fruition. The Inn opened in 1930 as the Northland Hotel. During its heyday, it played host to many famous visitors including Amelia Earhart, Abbott and Costello, Maya Angelou, Louis Armstrong, Bill Cosby, Jim Harrison, Duke Ellington, the Rolling Stones, Jimmy Stewart, Lee Remick, and George C. Scott (these latter three when they were in Marquette filming *Anatomy of a Murder*).

Shortly after the Inn opened, the first ghost story emerged. A gentleman, who sailed on one of the ships that regularly stopped at Marquette Harbor, began staying at the opulent hotel during his shore leave. While in the city, the sailor also frequented the local library, and there he met a librarian and struck up a friendship that blossomed into a love affair. After several months of courting, he asked for his lady love's hand in marriage. She accepted and made wedding plans. The couple discussed the long separations necessitated by the man's sailing career, and they decided he would retire from the lakes and become a landlubber. Before departing for his last trip aboard his ship, the sailor gave notice to his employer so his position could be filled with no hardship to his boss. The day the sailor was scheduled to return to port, the librarian went to the Landmark Inn to wait for him.

Before the lovers could be reunited, the fickle Michigan weather spat a storm that sank the man's ship. When the librarian learned of the tragedy, she tied a rope of lilac embellished napkins and hung herself outside the window of the Lilac Room. Her spirit remains on the sixth floor of the Landmark Inn where she continues to mourn her loss and perhaps hopes to somehow reverse fate.

<<>>

The Ghost of the Spurned Lover. A second Landmark Inn Ghost story tells the tale of a couple whose relationship turned sour. They sat in a bar one evening, and the woman, who had been drinking and having second thoughts about the liaison, began taunting her boyfriend.

"I cannot contemplate a marriage built on lies. You may not be man enough to keep me happy," she said.

The shocked man scarcely believed his ears. He asked her to repeat what she had said.

"I need excitement in my life, or at least a real man—one who makes me yearn for only him."

"What is it ya say? I've been kind and generous. I treat ya better than any of the blokes ya used to run with."

"Maybe that's the point. I've been seeing those blokes. I've missed their manliness."

"What have ya done? Do I have to worry about ya bein' unfaithful?"

"It's too late to worry about it. It's fact. So long as it don't bother you that I see others, I find no reason we can't still be married."

"Ya meanin' I provide the security, and they provide the thrills?"

"I wouldn't have put it that way."

The scorned man grabbed the woman by her wrist and dragged her outside and across the street to the construction site of the hotel. There the two stood in the dim light, silent and motionless as statues gracing the Northland Hotel property. The moon glistened off the inky water of the lake in the distance. The man, who seemed to be in a trance, bent over and picked up a cinder block. Holding it with both hands, he raised the chunk of concrete above his head and brought it crashing to the skull of the woman who until an hour earlier had been his sweetheart.

Realizing what he had done to the two-timing cheat, he thought for the first time of consequences. He shouldn't spend his life in prison because of a jealous rage, he thought. It was the wench's fault. Self-preservation claimed him. He slung the woman's lifeless body over his shoulder and carried her to the half-finished basement of the hotel. He covered the corpse with dirt.

The next day construction workers poured concrete, but as they did so, they reported hearing the cries of a woman begging them to uncover her final resting place. Her ghost continues wandering the area seeking justice.

<<>>

Amelia Earhart's Ghost. Earhart stayed at the Landmark Inn in 1932. Why she visited Marquette isn't clear, but she stayed in room 502. It is rumored that sometimes Earhart's ghost makes a visit to the room named after her. Why she is drawn to the place is a mystery.

<<>>

The Ghost of Beth Ann. *The Marquette Monthly* is a free arts and culture magazine that focuses on positive stories without stretching the truth to the breaking point. The publication's first issue dates back to 1999, but the two-story dwelling that houses the enterprise on Marquette's Third Street has a much longer history interlaced with happenstance and tragedy. Prior to purchase by *The Marquette Monthly*, the house in its early years was home to a young married couple. The wife, Beth Ann, operated a small printing office from the top floor. Her products met the stationery needs of local businesses. Publishing or printing was the lifeblood of the building.

In the course of Beth Ann's duties, she typeset, unclogged paper jams from feeders, and inked the machines. To a logical way of thinking, it wasn't a dangerous occupation, and it provided the woman with a diversion and way to augment the couple's income.

Alone in the shop one afternoon, Beth Ann struggled to clear a card stock jam as the machine drew the jam closer and closer and closer to the letterpress. She had handled clogs as a routine matter, but this time her billowy blouse sleeve caught and held her close enough to the feeder that she couldn't reach the power switch.

Her screams pierced the air. No help was within hearing distance, and Beth Ann was pulled into the savage machine. Her arm was severed before the machine shut down under the pressure of ripping her limb from its socket. Beth Ann slumped to the floor unconscious. She bled to death. Her husband returned from work late that night and found his wife separated from her arm, and the floor awash in her blood.

Beth Ann's horrific, unearthly screams are still heard in the darkest hours of the night.

<<>>

Ghosts of the Old Catholic Cemetery. Catholicism held a firm grip in the religious firmament of the U.P. It wasn't long after the first settlers arrived in Marquette that a need for a cemetery presented itself. Land was dedicated near the intersection of County Road 553 and Pioneer Road to provide a final resting place for Catholic believers. The earliest grave markers date to the mid-1800s. Burial in the cemetery was free, and it provided sites for many young women who died in childbirth, oftentimes a resting place for their infants as well.

By the beginning of the twentieth century, Holy Cross Catholic Cemetery on Wright Street opened, and the bodies from the Old Catholic Cemetery were moved to the new location. According to locals, many of the old graves could not be found, and the spirits of those left behind rise and demand to be given their final peace. While no particular ghost story has become urban legend, the cumulative sinister and spooky thought of disquieted ghosts make wandering the site at night a venture for only the stoutest of heart.

<<>>

Ghost of the Marquette Harbor Lighthouse. Located at 300 North Lakeshore and part of the Maritime Museum (See Museums), the Lighthouse is haunted by the ghost of a small girl who stares from the upper floor window of the lighthouse. Little is known or shared about this ghost who seemingly likes to look out on her beloved Lake Superior. While many ghosts only make appearances during the dark of night, this child favors sunshine. If you visit the lighthouse, you may see her anytime during the day.

<<>>

Several buildings on the Northern Michigan Campus house ghosts—or at least ghost stories.

Forest Roberts Theater Elevator. A portly janitor named Perry worked in the Forest Roberts Theater. One night, he succumbed to a massive heart attack in the elevator that connected the theater with the Thomas Fine Arts Building. Perry was good-natured and loved being around the students for whom he always had a kind word. After death he decided to stay in the midst of the action and haunts not only the elevator but both the theater and fine arts buildings.

<<>>

John X Jamrich Building. Purportedly a nursing student who haunted the old Jamrich building still shows her face in the control room window of the new 500-seat lecture hall that features a prominent stage. Why she is one of the unsettled dead is unclear.

<<>>

Halverson Hall, Room 304. The story claims a young girl came to visit a friend at Halverson Hall. Something—exactly what, no one seems certain—went horribly wrong, and she hung herself. Her ghost never left the place that caused her such emotional agony, and she can be seen wandering the third-floor hall.

13. Big Bay Point

Big Bay is a small town—even by small town standards. The 2020 population was 308, down from 319 a decade earlier. It lies on Lake Superior's southern coastline between Marquette and L'Anse in the Northern Upper Peninsula.

While the courthouse in Marquette was used for the trial in the 1959 movie, *Anatomy of a Murder*, other scenes were filmed at the Thunder Bay Inn and at the Big Bay Lighthouse Bed and Breakfast in Big Bay. The town's Lumberjack Tavern, the location of the real-life crime that inspired the book, was also the setting for the murder scene in the movie.

Lieutenant Coleman Peterson was a veteran of the Korean War and an active member of the 768th Antiaircraft Artillery Training Battalion camped in a meadow west of the Big Bay lighthouse. Peterson believed his wife Charlotte Ann was raped by barkeeper Mike Chenoweth. To avenge Charlotte's rape, Peterson shot and killed Chenoweth. (For additional information, see Books and Movies with Ties to Marquette.)

If you are following Michigan's waterway borders, you'll pass Big Bay, and you may wish to stop at a local restaurant or curio shop. Or maybe take advantage of two noteworthy scenic stops. If you drive through at night, be forewarned, Big Bay is also home to unsettled ghosts.

• Other Stops to Consider

Thomas Rock Scenic Overlook, 505 Loop, is an often-missed gem that is especially beautiful during the fall color tour. The trails are well-marked and easy to maneuver with only gentle inclines. The view of Big Bay is worth the hike.

<<>>

Yellow Dog Falls, County Road 510, is not too far from Thomas Rock Scenic Overlook. This series of falls is off the beaten path and less touted than its better-known brother and sister falls, but it is also more secluded and peaceful. Like Thomas Rock, the optimal time to visit is during the Fall Color Tour. Take lots of bug spray. There is a small parking lot, but that's it for amenities.

• Lighthouses

Big Bay Point Lighthouse stands on a rocky point halfway between Marquette and Keweenaw Portage Entry. The Lighthouse Board recommended the establishment of a lighthouse at this location in 1892 because this was the spot where steamers had to change course which brought additional danger. Congress approved $25,000 for lighthouse construction. A five-acre parcel of land was acquired for the project. In late 1896, the lighthouse was completed. A two-unit house, one for the main keeper and one for the assistant, was built for those servicing the lighthouse. In 1941 the last keeper left. In 1961 the lighthouse was decommissioned. Today the dwelling is privately owned and operated as a B&B. The property is reportedly haunted. (See Ghost Stories.)

<<>>

Huron Island Light stands offshore from Bay Point in the Huron Islands Wilderness. The lighthouse was constructed in 1868 to warn freighters away from dangerous shoals. The risk from those shoals was often increased by fog. The lighthouse was automated in 1972 and remains an aid to navigation. Huron Island Light was added to the National Register of Historic Places in 1975. The United States Fish and Wildlife Service currently owns the lighthouse which is only accessible by tour or private boat. If you want to use the latter, you are warned to exercise care. Although the island is only three miles from the mainland, the way is sprinkled with obstacles, and the lake is cold and treacherous.

• Ghost Stories

William Prior's Ghost. According to the stories told about him, Prior was a cantankerous and difficult man. A red-haired, ill-tempered individual especially well-suited to the lonely life of lighthouse keeper at Big Bay Point.

Much of what is known of Prior is recorded in his meticulous records. He arrived with his family in August of 1896. Hardship and tragedy became Prior's companions for the next five years. His journal doesn't dwell on good times—he never mentions them—but it captures the turmoil between this head keeper and the assistants sent to work with him.

The first, Ralph Heater, finally escaped his misery through a transfer to Granite Island. It was obvious from Prior's notes that he found Heater unsatisfactory, lazy, and unduly influenced by a wife without a work ethic. The next assistants were no more favored by Prior who complained of problems with one after another.

In 1899 William's son, George, began taking on an assistant's duties. In January 1900, George was officially appointed assistant. It appears that the son did everything he could to please his demanding father.

George was injured when he plummeted down the steep, narrow lighthouse steps splitting the skin of his upper leg to his femur. So worried about incurring his father's wrath or inviting a diatribe about his carelessness, George minimized the accident and wasn't immediately taken for medical attention. He tried to work in spite of the injury. When it became apparent the son's leg—swollen and red and hot—would not heal, the father sought medical attention for his injured boy. The fastest way to Marquette where medical facilities awaited was by rowboat. William, now believing his son was seriously ill, rowed as fast as he could. But infectious poisons ate away at George's body. After two months of grotesque suffering, George succumbed to septicemia.

William, beset with guilt and anguish, disappeared into the woods one day. His wife Mary couldn't account for his whereabouts, and local citizens attempted to find him without success. Mary packed up her four younger children and moved to Marquette.

Eighteen months later, a hunter found a body hanging from a tree. He brought others back with him, and the small group noted the clothes hanging from the skeleton were consistent with those of a lighthouse keeper. The death could have been murder, but it is believed the despondency William suffered after his son's death drove him to take his own life.

In the middle of the night, a red-haired specter walks the lighthouse property. A vision of this apparition is seen in mirrors, and sometimes doors bang shut without the help of human hand or wind. It is believed to be William paying penance for actions he took that contributed to the tragedy. Actions that he could not undo.

<<>>

Ghosts at the Thunder Bay Inn. In 1943 Henry Ford purchased 313,000 acres of timberland in the Upper Peninsula for logging. His purpose was to find more efficient ways to manufacture automobiles with materials solely within his control. At the time, his cars had wooden panels on the doors. Ford established remote mills in several places including Big Bay. Big Bay was unusual, however. There he bought the sawmill, the power plant, and nearby houses and from them created a company town. The current Thunder Bay Inn was built in 1911 and served as a functioning depot, first aid station, and storage site for the mill across the street. The building was converted by Ford to a hotel in the 1940s. Henry and his wife Clara enjoyed their time in Big Bay where their property became a destination for Ford executives. But the venture couldn't turn a profit, and in 1951 Henry abandoned it.

Ghost hunters and other paranormal enthusiasts claim to get ghostly vibes at the Inn. One theory is that Ford's guests enjoyed the experience so much that they come back in the afterlife for another vacation. A rocking chair that moves on its own without any breeze, fan, or human assistance has led to speculation that a ghostly parent continues to rock its child.

<<>>

Cabin 13 at Bay Cliff Health Camp. A year-round camp for children and adults with physical disabilities, Bay Cliff is said to be haunted. The camp was established in 1934 to provide for the needs of malnourished or otherwise neglected children during the Great Depression when many families suffered financial ruin. By the 1940s, the number of children suffering as a result of the depression had lessened, and the focus of Bay Cliff turned to helping children afflicted with polio. In the next decade, the service widened to include children with a variety of impairments.

According to urban legend, a young boy named Sam came to the camp. Instead of finding like-minded friends and a supportive staff, he was bullied. Sam was more interested in his artwork and intellectual pursuits than nature. He wore thick, coke-bottle glasses and cared little about his appearance. He was assigned to cabin 13 and became the brunt of serious intimidation that included destroying his artwork and stomping on his glasses.

Unable to escape the taunts of his peers, and without glasses that allowed him to paint, Sam fell into a deep abiding depression and decided to end his life. The camp didn't provide him with an easy means to accomplish that goal. He resorted to a sharp-tipped feather pen which he gruesomely used to puncture a vein. Today's campers tell stories of heavy paintings falling during the night. Awakened and curious, they try to rehang the art, but the pictures float upward and rehang themselves. Campers have also sought medical treatment for glass they stepped on in Cabin 13 when nothing was known to have broken there. It is rumored the glass bits are recurring vestiges of Sam's glasses.

14. L'Anse

This village, 2020 population of 2,019, is located on the southern end of L'Anse Bay, part of the larger Keweenaw Bay, in Lake Superior. It was home to the Lake Superior Band of Ojibwe long before the French and other Europeans came to the area. The name L'Anse means cove or bay in French.

Honored as the Town Father of L'Anse, Pierre Crebassa, built an American Fur Trading Post at the present-day L'Anse Township Park just north of L'Anse. Crebassa wrote to and convinced Father Baraga to join him and build a Catholic Mission in the area. Crebassa became the first area postmaster in 1866. The mission was built in nearby Baraga. Later day L'Anse grew around the early trading post.

By nineteenth century treaties, the Ojibwe relinquished extensive parcels of land to the United States government. The L'Anse Indian Reservation they retained is the largest and oldest in Michigan.

A railroad line that ended at the head of Keweenaw Bay, along with stagecoach and boat travel, allowed the small town to boom. Businesses were established there, an iron ore dock was built, and L'Anse was expected to grow more successful than Marquette or Escanaba.

It didn't happen. L'Anse fell on hard times when the panic of 1873, caused in part by speculation and rapid railroad expansion, created a financial crisis in North America.

On May 9, 1896, L'Anse suffered further hardship when a fire started in the L'Anse Lumber Company sawmill. Dry conditions and strong winds drove the conflagration through the small community, destroyed everything in its path, and left many residents homeless. Assistance came from neighboring communities, and the village rebuilt but never to the standards of earlier dreams.

• TRAIL AND WATERFALL

Canyon Falls Trail, US 41. The falls are a short walk of a little over a mile from the rest stop parking lot. Your hiking efforts are rewarded with views of a series of waterfalls and rapids that carry the Sturgeon River through a scenic box canyon of flat rock. If it's a hot day and you have a swimsuit with you, you may be enticed to do some cliff-diving.

• GHOST TOWN

Pequaming doesn't boast spirits or specters but rather claims to be the largest ghost town in the Upper Peninsula. Located about five miles north of L'Anse, the Lakeshore Road takes you into the center of the former village. The name Pequaming came from the Odawe word *Pequaquawaming* which means the headland. It referred to a narrow strip of land almost surrounded by water. The point at Pequaming is shaped like a bear; the head is called Picnic Point, the tail is at the lumberyard, the legs are the two sand beaches, and the back is the shoreline.

Pequaming Ghost Town. Courtesy of Pixabay Free Images.

A lumber company began business there in the late 1870s and became wildly successful—the largest lumbering and milling operation in the Upper Peninsula. Henry Ford purchased the mill and the surrounding town it in the 1920s. He turned it into what he believed was a perfect company town just as he had done at Big Bay Point. And like at Big Bay Point, his goal was to have lumber available nearby to fill his need for wood panel doors on his automobiles. By the end of WWII, Ford discontinued the use of wood panel doors. He no longer needed Pequaming, and the city fell into decline. By the 1960s, most of the large structures from the manufacturing process were torn down because they were feared to be attractive nuisances. The pier, water tower, schoolhouse, general store, and shell of the abandoned Ford factory remain. A mere shadow of its former self, Pequaming is a remnant of the Upper Peninsula's former prosperity.

Time comes full circle, and Pequaming, which became a ghost town with a only a few straggling citizens, now shows signs of reawakening. New residents, often folks seeking a second home in a quiet scenic area, are building homes and moving to Pequaming. A pleasant bicycle ride from L'Anse, this is a place to step back and connect with history.

15. Baraga

The village of Baraga, with a 2020 population of 2,102, opened a post office in 1869 and was called Bristol. Less than a year later the name was changed to Baraga to honor Bishop Frederic Baraga who established Holy Name Mission at the site. Baraga is less than four miles from L'Anse, and the two villages share much of their history. Bishop Baraga was drawn to the area by Pierre Crebassa, the founder of L'Anse, who wanted the priest to open a mission.

• Museum

Baraga County Historical Museum, 803 US 41. Operated by the Historical Society, the goal of the museum is to collect, preserve, and display artifacts and documents connected to Baraga County's cultural heritage and natural resources.

The museum features a letter written by Bishop Baraga to a local founding father, logging tools, antique children's toys, military memorabilia, glassware, household items, artwork of locals, and official indexes to recorded births, deaths, and marriages in Baraga County from 1875 through approximately 1970. The museum has both temporary and permanent exhibits and displays a headdress belonging to Herbert Welsh, the grandson of Chief Sitting Bull. Check for hours if you plan to visit the museum.

• Beaches, Parks, and Trails

Baraga State Park, 1300 US 41 South. Camping, showers, kids' activities. Campsites are on the smallish side, and some visitors complain about noise from the nearby highway.

<<>>

Lower Silver Falls. The cascading water is pleasant to watch, but this is not a major waterfall. A rough dirt road, more appropriate for jeeps, motorcycles, and dirt bikes than luxury vehicles, gets you there. The path is studded with rocks and tree branches. The upside is uncrowded space to enjoy the views. If you are going through Baraga and need an excuse for a hike, or you're looking for solitude and a quiet place to eat your lunch, check it out.

• Another Stop to Consider

Bishop Baraga Shrine, 17570 US 41. A 35-foot bronze statue weighing over four tons overlooks the Keweenaw Bay of Lake Superior. Father Baraga was known as the snowshoe priest. The figure holds a 7-foot cross and 26-foot snowshoes. Father Baraga spent 38 years traveling hundreds of miles each winter by snowshoe to minister to his flock.

Bishop Baraga Statue.
Courtesy of Pixabay Free Images.

• Lighthouse

Sand Point (Baraga) Lighthouse. In 1863 a committee was dispatched to the Great Lakes to determine the necessity of additional lighthouses and the possibility of reestablishing discontinued lights to make Lake Superior water travel safer. The committee determined that a lighthouse was needed to support additional ship traffic connected to the growing copper and iron ore trade near the Keweenaw Peninsula. A light at Sand Point at the entrance to L'Anse Bay was one of the committee's recommendations.

Congress provided $10,000 on March 3, 1873, for a lighthouse at L'Anse. It took an additional three years to obtain a suitable parcel of land, and construction was delayed until August 1877. The red brick lighthouse had a tower with lantern room, and two floors with a total of five rooms for the keeper's dwelling.

The Sand Point Lighthouse was sold when it was no longer needed. It was purchased by the Keweenaw Bay Indian Community for use as office space. The historical significance of the lighthouse is recognized. Restoration attempts and reopening the lighthouse to the public are the goals.

16. HOUGHTON

Houghton, 2020 population of 7,947, and Hancock, 2020 population of 4,547, are located on US 41. They are the main cities in the Keweenaw Peninsula. They are not on the Lake Superior shoreline, and they are not geographically part of the St. Lawrence Seaway or Michigan's waterway borders. Yet they provide freighters traveling Lake Superior with a shortcut to avoid the often-tempestuous waters around the Keweenaw Peninsula. With that nexus, and because you will likely drive through them on your way to the Keweenaw Peninsula or Isle Royale, they are included here.

With the surge of copper mining, both towns prospered. Portage Lake and the Portage River provided the larger part of a natural water pathway across the Keweenaw Peninsula, dividing it almost in half. In the 1860s, a ship canal was built connecting Portage Lake on the east to Lake Superior on the west. The completion of the canal technically turned the upper portion of the Keweenaw Peninsula into an island, but if you were to ask a Michigander where Copper Harbor is, they would tell you it's at the tip of the Keweenaw Peninsula, not on Keweenaw Island. In an earlier time, the Finnish in the area referred to this area as Copper Island, since it is separated from land by water on all sides.[2] Neither the United States

---

[2] Island: Noun. A piece of land surrounded on all sides by water. Peninsula: noun. a piece of land *almost* surrounded by water or projecting out into a body of water. So, is this area of Keweenaw north of Hougton-Hancock an island or a peninsula?

Geological Survey nor the State of Michigan identifies this area as an island. Perhaps that is because it was not naturally an island but ended up separated from contiguous land by a manmade canal. If classified as an island, it would be the largest island in the state with 554 square miles. Since Keweenaw remains identified as a peninsula, the largest island status goes to Isle Royale, the largest naturally isolated island in Lake Superior.

The name Keweenaw comes from the Ojibwe word meaning portage. Before the canal, canoes had to be portaged part of the way across the peninsula. Once the canal opened, ships could travel through the Keweenaw Waterway, and large vessels could anchor at Houghton and Hancock. The Keweenaw Waterway also provided ships with a Harbor of Refuge from Superior's violent storms.

On opposite sides of the river, and with such similar histories, the cities of Houghton and Hancock seem joined at the hip, the hip being the narrow end of Portage Lake with Houghton on the south and Hancock on the north. They are often spoken of as parts of one unit as in, "I'm going to Houghton-Hancock."

A bridge to connect Houghton to Hancock was built in 1875. Major repairs were needed in 1905. The current double deck Portage Lake Lift Bridge, built in 1959, is the heaviest aerial lift bridge in the world. The upper deck is for vehicular traffic. Pedestrians and snowmobiles can use the lower bridge. The lower level was originally intended for trains, but when the tracks were no longer needed, they were removed. The bridge is the only land entrance to the tip of the Keweenaw Peninsula. As connected as they are, the cities of Houghton and Hancock are each unique.

Houghton, different from Houghton Lake which is in the lower peninsula, is the largest city and the county seat of Houghton County. It was included by Norman Crampton in his book, *The 100 Best Small Towns in America*. City and county were named in honor of Douglass Houghton, an

American geologist and a physician whose career focus was exploring the Keweenaw Peninsula.

For thousands of years before French fur traders discovered wealth in the fur-bearing animals, Native Americans mined copper in and around what would later become Houghton. After the fur trade dwindled, Europeans discovered that copper was the way to riches. Cornish and Finnish immigrants arrived to work in the mines.

From 1913 to 1914, there were strikes by copper workers seeking higher pay and shorter hours. By October 1913, mine owners requested that the governor send in the National Guard to quell the strikes and related upheaval. The presence of troops escalated the violence. The greatest of the strike's tragedies occurred on Christmas Eve while mine workers celebrated the holiday in the Italian Hall in nearby Calumet. The strike was, at that time, in its fifth month. During the celebration someone yelled "fire." With only a narrow, steep stairway for egress, 73 people were killed, most of them children. Woody Guthrie memorialized the tragedy in his song, "1913 Massacre," which suggests that mine bosses held the door shut so when the panicked partygoers reached the bottom of the stairway, they couldn't escape. Other theories claim the doors to the outside opened inward, and the crowd pressed so tightly against them that no one could break out. At least two books have been written about the disaster, and historians still debate the circumstances. The strike ended in April 1914.

MTU Mascot. Courtesy of Bob Royce.

Houghton is home to Michigan Technological University established in 1855 as Michigan College of Mines to teach Metallurgy and Mine Engineering. The mines are gone, but the university is going strong and is the largest employer in the area.

Professional ice hockey was born in Houghton in 1903 when the Portage Lakers Hockey Team formed. If you ask a resident of Houghton how many seasons they have, you are likely to be told, "Two. Winter. And Winter's Coming.

• Museums

The **A.E. Seaman Mineral Museum of Michigan**, 1404 East Sharon Ave on the campus of Michigan Technological University, is a stop appreciated by rock hounds. The museum was opened in 1902 and named for professor Arthur Edmund Seaman who worked at the university. The museum has more than 25,000 specimens from around the world, with emphasis on minerals from Michigan, especially the Lake Superior Region. The displays are well-organized, clearly labeled, and beautiful. You can examine Calcite, Rhodochrosite, Azurite, Spessartine, Sulfur, and Pyromorphite samples among the collection.

<<>>

The **Carnegie Museum of the Keweenaw**, 105 Huron Street, built with grant funding from Andrew Carnegie, was home to the Portage Lake District Library for nearly a century before the library moved and the building opened as a museum in 2006. Built in the Classical Revival Style, the structure is on the National Register of Historic Places. History students and professors at MTU are working to expand the museum which offers year-round exhibits, videos, and speakers focused on Houghton and the Keweenaw area.

• The Famous or Infamous with Ties to Houghton

Nancy Harkness Love was born in 1914 in Houghton. Her passion for aviation led her to a career in the U.S. Air Force where she served as a World War II commander and pilot. She ended her service with the rank of Lieutenant Colonel.

<<>>

P.J. Olsson, lead singer for the Alan Parsons Live Project, was born July 13, 1969, in Houghton.

<<>>

The list of notables from the Houghton-Hancock area is heavy on hockey players. It includes **Herb Boxer** who played hockey with the Detroit Red Wings, **Paul Coppo** an Olympic and professional hockey player, **Ralph Heikkinen**, **Dwight Helminen**, **Ike Klingbeil**, **Joseph Linder**, **Eddie Olson**, **Rodney Paavola**, and **Bruce Riutta**.

17. Hancock

Hancock is consistently rated one of the snowiest cities in the United States because of the lake effect on the frozen precipitation. It is not unusual for the city to be blanketed with more than an annual 300 inches. One year 364 inches were recorded, and 200 inches seems pretty normal. You can expect snow at least 90 days a year. The Weather Channel says you might want to hibernate like an overly drowsy bear cub if you live in the Houghton-Hancock area. The Weather Channel would be wrong. Residents of the area celebrate all winter long with skiing and snow festivals.

The history of Hancock is mining. Copper became a mainstay of the economy in 1848 when a group of prospectors discovered a series of prehistoric Ojibwe copper mining pits. They named the hillside of their found treasure Quincy Hill. The 100 feet of pits became the Quincy Mining Company which received a special charter by the state legislature to carry on mining activities.

The city was named for John Hancock, a signer of the Declaration of Independence. Bishop Baraga left his mark on the area. He was given a parcel of land at the corner of current-day Quincy and Ravine to construct a church.

Originally part of Portage Charter Township, Hancock was organized into the new township of Hancock on April 1, 1861, and on March 10, 1863, the Village of Hancock was officially organized. Seven years later Hancock was consumed by a horrific fire when a local saloon exploded as the result of a defective stovepipe. Wind gusts drove the flames throughout the village, leveling 150 buildings including every store and nearly all businesses, the wooden bridges, and 120 homes. There was no fire department to quell the blaze.

• Park and Trail

McLain State Park, 18350 Highway M-203, open year-round with campsites and cabins. Four miles of hiking or cross-country skiing trails include flat woodlands and hills. Visitors come for fishing, beachcombing, and windsurfing. It's a place to get a great view of the lighthouse (See Lighthouse section.) and enjoy a spectacular sunset.

• Other Stops to Consider

The Copper Country Community Arts Center (CCCAC), 126 Quincy Street, provides gallery space for artists to display and sell their work. By supporting local artists, the Center enriches the culture of the area. The Center runs a working letterpress studio, clay studio, and black and white photography darkroom. You can visit the Center's three galleries—the Kerredge with monthly artist exhibitions, the Youth Gallery featuring artwork by local schools and young artists, and the Artists Market Sales Gallery which showcases the art of more than 170 local and regional artists.

<<>>

The **Finnish-American Heritage Centre and the Finnish-American National Historical Archive**, 435 Quincy

Street, houses a comprehensive collection of Finnish-American history. The Center is dedicated to preserving and celebrating Finnish culture and life.

<<>>

Quincy Mine, part of the Keweenaw National Historical Park, 49750 US 41 outside Hancock, sits atop Quincy Hill. Among the surviving structures is the 1918 Nordberg Steam Hoist, the world's largest steam-powered hoist engine. It once lowered the copper miners into the mine shaft. Visitors can take an underground or surface tour with a tram ride and relive the mining history of the Keweenaw Peninsula.

• LIGHTHOUSE

The **Keweenaw Waterway Upper Entrance Light** is located at the north end of the Portage River and can be viewed from McLain State Park. It was listed on the National Register of Historic Places in 2014. After dredging in 1860 to make the Portage River accessible to larger ships, it was necessary to mark the mouth of the waterway by a lighthouse. The first light was constructed in 1874 atop a nearby bluff. Ongoing improvements extended two piers into Lake Superior to offer greater protection to the entrance to the river. The current light is stationed four-tenths of a mile offshore on a rock-filled, steel-supporting structure. A single-story octagonal concrete fog signal building has a 50-foot-tall steel light tower topped with a light automated in 1970.

18. COPPER HARBOR

The 2020 population of Copper Harbor, a census-designated place, was 71. It's a destination tailored to bring smiles to the faces of rugged adventurers riding mountain bikes or driving 4-wheelers. The area attracts campers and hardy outdoor types, not those looking for an upscale resort. Activities require a heavy dose of insect repellent. For most trails and nature areas, you'll be happy to have sturdy shoes, and it wouldn't hurt to have a walking stick.

Located at the tip of the Keweenaw Peninsula, Copper Harbor, like most other points in the U.P., was originally home to the Ojibwe who lived there for centuries before Europeans arrived in North America.

By treaties, including the 1836 Treaty of Washington, Native Americans ceded much of what is now the Upper Peninsula to the United States. The 1836 deal, brokered by Indian Agent Henry Schoolcraft, provided for additional changes to treaty terms after the Native American representatives left the proceedings. The Native Americans were promised permanent reservation lands and perpetual access to natural resources, including hunting and fishing rights, and the guarantee of additional services, plus a certain price for the land.

The Ojibwe and Odawa had barely begun their back to the U.P. before congress altered the treaty. Permanent rights turned into five years which Schoolcraft then suggested be reduced to two years followed by forceful removal. The tribes waged a successful legal battle against removal.

Copper Harbor, site of the first mineral land agency in the Lake Superior District, saw the Pittsburgh and Boston Copper Harbor Mining Company open operations in 1844. Other mining companies followed. So aggressive was mining that by 1870 the area was largely depleted of copper.

An interesting snippet of trivia: Highway US 41 begins in Copper Harbor and ends 2,000 miles south in Miami, Florida.

• Museums

Fort Wilkins Historic State Park, 15223 US 41, Copper Harbor. The fort, built on the shores of Lake Fanny Hooe in

1844, was intended to bring law and order to the area and protect the booming copper mining industry. Troops stationed at Fort Wilkins helped local law enforcement maintain peace for the miners who feared violence as a result of Native American dissatisfaction with treaties. The effort was born more of paranoia than from necessity. The Native Americans and the miners all remained law-abiding.

Originally the Army build 27 structures including a guardhouse, powder magazine, seven officers' quarters, two barracks, two mess halls, a hospital, storehouse, sutler's store, quartermaster's store, bakery, blacksmith's shop, carpenter's shop, icehouse, stables, slaughterhouse, and quarters for married enlisted men. Fourteen of the fort's original buildings have been restored and living history demonstrations are held in them.

Winter was a desolate time for men stationed here. No ships got through and icy cold weather was the norm. In 1923 the fort and lighthouse (See Lighthouse Section.) became part of the state park and are operated by the Michigan Department of Natural Resources.

Fort Wilkins. Courtesy of Bob Royce.

The fort was placed on the National Register of Historic Places in 1970 and may be one of the most interesting stops of your Lake Superior travels. Camping facilities are available.

<<>>

Steve Brimm Earthworks Factory, 216 First Street. Brimm is a well-respected and talented photographer whose studio is a favorite with travelers.

• Beaches, Parks, and Trails

Brockway Mountain Drive is an almost nine-mile route that follows a high ridge between the communities of Copper Harbor and Eagle Harbor. It has been called the most beautiful road in Michigan.

Never let it be said that Michigan doesn't have a heart for romance. Watching the sunset from Brockway Mountain is as enchanting as it gets. There is a story that says if you kiss your beloved just as the sun disappears in the West, your relationship will be long and loving. However, even if you only have eyes for each other, don't let the view go unappreciated. Lake Superior never looked better.

<<>>

Copper Harbor Bicycle Trail System, a network of more than 35 miles of challenging trails with something appropriate for all skill levels. For the past 20 years, these trails have earned a reputation as a mountain biking destination. Your ride takes you past rocky outgrowths, ridges, valleys, old-growth forests, historic locations, inland lakes, streams, mountains, and the rugged Lake Superior shoreline. Trail maps are available online and locally.

<<>>

Estivant Pines Nature Sanctuary on Clark Mine Road can be accessed from Burma Road. This 508-acre wilderness offers hiking trails from which you may spot 85 species of birds native to the sanctuary. You will walk through cedars, balsam, sugar maples, and the largest expanse of old-growth Eastern White Pines in Michigan, some of which are 500 years old, measure five feet in diameter, and stand 125 feet tall.

<<>>

High Rock Bay, M-42 north of Fort Wilkins. Caution: This is not appropriate for regular vehicles unless you want to call a tow truck to haul you out. For those adventurous souls driving a tough vehicle with a high undercarriage, you will be rewarded with perfect vistas of Manitou Island and perhaps a quiet walk along the beach. Bring a picnic lunch but don't expect amenities.

<<>>

Horseshoe Harbor Nature Conservancy, US 41 north past Copper Harbor. Keep driving until the pavement turns to gravel, then dirt, and then to a small parking lot from which it is a walk to the purple stone Horseshoe Harbor and a beach appreciated by rockhounds. The bay is framed on either side by ancient bedrock of Copper Harbor Conglomerate that contains volcanic rock mixed with sedimentary. This area around the bay is the Mary McDonald Preserve, and it is run by the Nature Conservancy.

<<>>

Hunter's Point Park, just west of Copper Harbor, is a narrow sliver of land that tries mightily to protect Copper Harbor from the storms of Lake Superior. The point is a flattish area that juts into Lake Superior from the west. It is named for an early resident who is buried in the Fort Wilkins Cemetery. Birders enjoy the park because migratory birds make a stop here. Rugged beauty is the standard in this area, and you'll encounter lots of it at this park. Rock hounds swear they are in heaven, but you can't take the rocks from this park home with you. Park trails are used both for hiking and in the winter for cross-country skiing.

<<>>

Lake Fanny Hooe, one mile east of Copper Harbor, runs parallel with M-26. The lake is two miles long, but only a quarter of a mile wide. It covers 227 acres, has a maximum depth of 40 feet, and borders Fort Wilkins. It connects by Garden Brook to Lake Superior. The Lake Fanny Hooe campground and resort offers swimming, fishing, a playground, and other amenities.

<<>>

Manganese Falls, US 41 east to Lake Manganese Road, turn right and go seven-tenths of a mile. The water comes through Lake Fanny Hooe and drops 20 feet into a gorge. The waterfall is partly hidden behind steep rock formations. There is a viewing platform that provides visitors with a partial peek looking straight at the crest and down the gorge.

• Another Stop to Consider

The **Copper Harbor Schoolhouse**, 346 Gratiot. Worth a drive-by since this is an operating one-room schoolhouse, and the most northern school in Michigan. Although it serves fewer pupils than you can count on your fingers, the quality of education is presumed good since 95% of the students go on to institutes of higher education.

• Lighthouses

Copper Harbor Light is located in the harbor inside Fort Wilkins Historic State Park. The lighthouse is a Michigan State Historic Site (1974) and also listed on the National Register of Historic Places (2012). Funding to build the light was approved in 1847, and the first tower constructed the next year. In 1866 the tower was dismantled and the stones were used to build a foundation for a replacement lighthouse. The actual light was removed from the lighthouse in 1933 and placed in a 62-foot-tall white tower with a range of 14 nautical miles. In 1957 the Coast Guard sold Copper Harbor Lighthouse to the State of Michigan for

$5,000. The state incorporated the historic lighthouse with Fort Wilkins State Park, and restorations efforts began. The lighthouse is not open to the public.

<<>>

Copper Harbor Front Range and Rear Range Lights, completed in 1869, added a layer of safety on either side for vessels traversing dangerous Lake Superior reefs as they entered the harbor. The original lighthouse illuminated the harbor but wasn't sufficient as a guide through the entry to the harbor. The range lights were electrified in 1937, and the keeper's dwelling eventually was used as the residence for the assistant manager of Fort Wilkins State Park.

• Shipwrecks

The **Keweenaw Underwater Preserve** stretches from the entry to the Keweenaw Waterway near Houghton-Hancock, along the coast of Lake Superior, past Eagle Harbor, and North to Copper Harbor. Artifacts from at least a dozen unlucky ships scatter this stretch and provide divers with opportunities for exploration: *Maplehurst, Tioga, James Pickands, William C. Moreland, John L. Gross, City of St. Joseph, John Jacob Astor, Wasaga, City of Superior, Mesquite*, and *Langham.* Of these the best dives are:

The ***Mesquite***, a U.S. Coast Guard Cutter, is considered the premier dive destination in the Underwater Preserve. A U.S. Naval Salvage report noted, "On 4 December 1989, the United States Coast Guard Buoy Tender *Mesquite* (WLB-305) stranded on a rock ledge while tending a light buoy in Lake Superior roughly one-half mile east southeast of Keweenaw Point, near Copper Harbor, Michigan. With the hold and motor room flooded, and five feet of water in the engine room, the crew abandoned ship and were rescued by a passing cargo vessel."

<<>>

The ***S.S. Tioga*** wrecked on Sawtooth Reef off Eagle River on November 26, 1919. She carried a cargo of grain from Superior, Wisconsin. The pilothouse broke free and floated into Eagle River. It has been restored and is currently exhibited at the Eagle River Museum.

<<>>

The ***City of St. Joseph***, a steamer, was in tow of the tug *John Roen* with the barge *Transport* when she was cut loose and forced ashore near Eagle Harbor. She was a total loss. One life was lost.

<<>>

The ***John Jacob Astor*** went down in 1844 near old Fort Wilkins and is believed to be the oldest ship in the preserve. Owned by Astor's American Fur Company, she struck a reef and foundered. The wreckage was still visible in the 1960s, and her anchor was found in 1970.

<<>>

The ***Langham***, a wooden steamer built in 1888, was lost to fire on October 23, 1910. The ship was loaded with coal and anchored in the Keweenaw Peninsula off Bete Grise Bay. The vessel burned to the waterline and settled in 105 feet of water.

<<>>

The ***Wasaga***, a wooden steamer, burned to a total loss on November 7, 1910. She went down with a cargo of farm equipment that can still be seen in the underwater preserve.

The dive sites of the preserve are not generally buoyed. The diving experience is enhanced by unique geological formations. (See Shipwrecks under Eagle Harbor.)

19. Isle Royale

Isle Royale was established as an American National Park on April 3, 1940. A designated wilderness area, it is protected from development and is a UNESCO International Biosphere Reserve. Located 45 miles north of Copper Harbor in Lake Superior, it is the northernmost and largest Michigan island, 45 miles long and nine miles wide at its widest point. This presumes you do not count the Keweenaw Peninsula which is divided from the remainder of the Upper Peninsula by the Houghton Waterway as an island. Isle Royale covers 209 square miles of land not including the surface area of 400 adjacent islands. Its landmass is greater than any of the 17 smallest countries in the world.

Mining activity began on the island as far back as 3,000 B.C. Later, in his journals of 1669-1670, Jesuit missionary Claude Dablon referenced the island and called it *Menong*, the name given to it by its indigenous population.

The Ojibwe relinquished their claim to Isle Royale in 1843 in an addendum to the La Pointe Treaty. Prior to the treaty, most Europeans on the island were fishermen or fur traders. After the treaty, copper mining began in earnest, but the efforts were disappointing. Most mining activity was curtailed by 1855.

Isle Royale is known for its timber wolf and moose populations which are of special interest to scientists studying the predator-prey relationship between the two animals. Over the past century, Isle Royale has established itself as an excellent location for such studies because of its closed environment where most mainland animals are not present.

Neither animal was indigenous to Isle Royale. The moose are believed to have swum across Lake Superior from Minnesota in the early 1900s or were brought to the island by man to create prey for recreational hunters. A pair of wolves crossed to the island during the particularly frigid winter of 1949 when the lake froze over from Ontario to the island. With only one original pair of wolves, there was inbreeding that threatened the colony on the island.

The moose population has ranged from 500 to 2,500 on the island during the last century, while the number of wolves had decreased from almost 50 down to 2. In 2018 wolves were released at Isle Royale in hopes of bringing back their population. In 2019 three new wolves, two males and one female, boosted the wolf population to 17. (See Books and Movies with Ties to Isle Royale if you are interested in additional information about the relationship between moose, wolves, and Isle Royale.)

You can travel to Isle Royale by ferry from either Houghton or Copper Harbor. (There is also service from Grand Portage, Minnesota.) Houghton offers a seaplane that gets you there in 30 minutes compared to the six-hour ferry service. You can also travel by personal boat. Isle Royale has become a chosen destination for wilderness enthusiasts and backpackers.

Three-sided wooden camping shelters and 36 locations for tent camping are available on the island. Rock Harbor Lodge provides visitors accommodations with private baths if they prefer a few amenities of civilization added to their wilderness experience. The Lodge has housekeeping cottages and a dining room. (See Rock Harbor under Beaches, Parks, and Trails.)

Isle Royale is the least visited National Park. When the National Park System took over management of the island, it bought the few cabins of the residents. They were given lifetime leases that weren't meant to be passed on to any family member who was unborn when the leases were granted. However, with the many islands and cabins that existed, the National Parks found it impossible to maintain all the cabins so the leases have continued for subsequent family members. These folks do not have a permanent leasehold. They are considered volunteers who maintain the small dwellings. According to the census, the island has no permanent residents. If getting away from it all is your goal, this destination is without roads, cars, or strip malls.

You are surrounded by miles of wilderness, chains of inland lakes to paddle and portage, and a rugged coastline that is best explored by kayak. Isle Royale offers hikers 165 miles of trails including some five-and-six-day treks across the entire length of the island. The island is open to visitors from mid-April to the end of October each year. Pets are not allowed on the island. Don't forget to take a compass. Streets are not laid out in a uniform grid.

• Museum

(See Rock Harbor Lighthouse.)

• Beaches, Parks, and Trails

Rock Harbor is the drop-off point for most ferries to the island. A good first stop is the visitor center. The store stocks basic provisions. Additional amenities include a lodge, cabins, restaurants, a gift shop, and water taxis to other parts of the island. You can refuel your private boat or rent kayaks and canoes. If you are lucky, a resident bull moose may be on hand to greet your arrival.

<<>>

Windingo is located in Washington Harbor at the southwest end of the island. You will find a store for basic supplies, a visitor center with a balcony for relaxing between adventures, and rustic one-room cabins without indoor plumbing, heat, or air-conditioning. The cabins include a picnic table and grill.

<<>>

Trails of Isle Royale. Greenstone Ridge Trail is the best-known trail and offers six routes ranging in length from four miles to 11.8 miles. Combining the trails allows you to traverse the entire island. Other trails include the Minong Ridge Trail, Feldtmann Ridge Trail, Rock Harbor Trail, Lake Richie Trail, Indian Portage Trail, Ishpeming Trail, East Chickenbone Trail, Hatchet Lake Trail, Tobin Harbor Trail,

Mt. Franklin Trail, Lane Cove Trail, Daisy Farm-Mt. Ojibwe Trails, Stoll Trail, Lookout Louise Trail, Inland Lakes South Trail, Raspberry Island Trail, Mott Island Circuit Trail, Lighthouse Loop Trail, Huginnin Cove Loop Trail, Windigo Nature Trail, and Rainbow Cove Trail. The numerous trails offer many choices and vary in difficulty and length. You can go online to get details about each route. You can also order a 184-page guide. (See Book with a Tie to Isle Royale.)

• Other Stops to Consider

Scoville Point is a rocky point that juts into Lake Superior with lovely views on either side. Often considered the best day hike from Rock Harbor, the hike is 4.2 miles each way.

<<>>

Lookout Louise. A steep, secluded hike that requires a canoe or water taxi. Views to the east are Duncan Bay, northwest views include Five Finger Bay and Belle Harbor, and views to the west are the Greenstone Ridge.

• Lighthouses

Rock Harbor Lighthouse. Built in 1855, this is the oldest lighthouse on Isle Royale. It has been restored and includes a small museum on the ground floor that provides an interesting history of shipwrecks in the area and keeper's memorabilia. The accessible tower provides a picturesque view of Lake Superior. The lighthouse is accessible by private or tour boat.

<<>>

Passage Island Light is located on a small island, off the east coast of Isle Royale. It is accessed by a ranger-guided tour arranged through Rock Harbor Lodge. The tour involves about an hour boat trip each way. The lighthouse was listed on the National Register of Historic Places in 2006.

Passage Island Lighthouse. Courtesy of Pixabay Free Images.

Rock of Ages Lighthouse. Courtesy of Lighthouse Photographer Gary Martin, www.coastalbeacons.com.

<<>>

Rock of Ages Light sits on a rock outcropping 3½ miles west of Isle Royale. It may be viewed by private boat or ferries from Isle Royale. Tourists may not be able to enter the light tower, but it is a favored site for taking pictures. Rock of Ages was automated in 1878 and remains an active aid to navigation.

• SHIPWRECKS

Isle Royale has claimed more than 25 ships on its treacherous reefs. Some were salvaged, others were too severely damaged to refloat them or reclaim parts or cargo. The two earliest ships that sank near Isle Royale were the *Madeline* (1839), and the American Fur Company's *Siskiwit* that went down a year later.

Neither the *Cumberland*, that went down in 1877, nor the bulk freighter, *Chester Congdon*, that sank in 1918, has been found.

Known as the three C ships of Isle Royale, the *Cumberland*, the *Henry Chisolm*, and the *George M. Cox* all succumbed to the Rock of Ages Reef.

<<>>

The ***Cumberland***, a passenger steamer, ran aground on the reef near Ontario before she made it to open lake. The trip that started with fine weather and a mild wind ended when the ship became stranded on Rock of Ages Reef. A salvage crew tried to free the ship, but the weather turned nasty before they completed their task. Today, battered by the elements for years, only scattered sections of her hull, sidewheel, and anchor remain on the reef.

<<>>

The ***Henry Chisolm*** was headed to Sault Ste. Marie in October 1898 when a storm separated her from a tow, the *Martin*. In the ensuing search for the *Martin*, the *Chisolm* ran aground on the reef. Like the *Cumberland*, salvage attempts were abandoned, and the *Chisolm* rests close to the *Cumberland*.

<<>>

The ***George M. Cox***, a 270-foot steamer, joined the *Cumberland* and the *Chisolm*, falling prey to the reef in May 1933. The foggy, but calm, lake befuddled the *Cox* as she headed for Fort William. Impact with the reef ripped her boilers loose and left the *Cox's* bow peering from high above the water. She settled just east of her sister ships. Crewmen evacuated the ship's passengers by life rafts and lifeboats, and the Rock of Ages lighthouse keeper was quick on the scene with his powerboat from which he towed the life rafts and lifeboats to shore. The 127 very cold passengers and crew spent the night in the lighthouse if they could find space. Other shivering souls spent the dark hours on the rocks around the lighthouse.

Divers can explore the three C ships doomed by the Rock of Ages Reef if they are willing to suffer the frigid water that gets as cold as 34° Fahrenheit.

<<>>

In addition to the three Cs and those mentioned above, six other shipwrecks at Isle Royale National Park have been listed on the National Register. These include the *Algoma, America, Emperor, Glenlyon, Kamloops*, and the *Monarch.*

<<>>

The **Ghost Ship S.S. *Bannockburn*** started her career with little fanfare. She was a cargo ship that passed through the Welland Locks, around the St. Lawrence Seaway, and into the Great Lakes. Little did she know that she would end her existence—or what we know of it—nicknamed the *Flying Dutchman* of *Lake Superior.*[3]

The *Bannockburn* was a workhorse that carried 1,500 tons of cargo. On November 20, 1902, she left Fort William headed for Georgian Bay. She ran aground shortly after the trip began, and that caused her to turn back to Fort William. The ship was carefully examined for damage, and with none apparent, she resumed her course the next day.

Captain James McMaugh of the upbound freighter *Algonquin* sighted the *Bannockburn* seven miles southeast of his position on November 21. He believed the

[3] The *Flying Dutchman* was a legendary ghost ship with a reputation for never making it to port, but rather, doomed to sail the oceans forever.

Bannockburn was about 80 miles off Keweenaw Point and 40 miles off Isle Royale. Captain McMaugh spotted the *Bannockburn* several additional times over the next few minutes. Then she disappeared into the fog. A violent storm crashed down on Lake Superior and at approximately 11:00 p.m., the passenger steamer, *Huronic*, observed the *Bannockburn* making good speed in the direction of the Soo Locks. The *Bannockburn* never arrived.

On November 25, the steamship *John D. Rockefeller*, sighted a debris field near Stannard Rock Light. The only ship missing, and the only ship whose remains that debris could be, was the *Bannockburn*. Five days later the *Bannockburn* was officially declared missing. Several days after that a lifejacket from the missing ship washed ashore near Grand Marias Lifesaving Station.

The *Bannockburn* did not disappear into obscurity like so many other ships before her. Sailors claim to have seen the *Bannockburn* with skeletons of the crew on deck. Just stories passed along and born of a bored sailor's imagination? Maybe and maybe not. Some of the tales are repeated by seamen who are respected for their veracity, and not known to be storytellers. For 119 years, there have been reports that on some nights before a major storm, ship crews see the *S.S. Bannockburn* sailing by in a fog or mist. Some believe sighting the *S.S. Bannockburn* is a bad omen.

• Books with Ties to Isle Royale

Jim DuFresne, ***Isle Royale National Park: Foot Trails & Water Routes***, is relied upon by backpackers to Isle Royale for complete descriptions of the trails and waterways including mileage, difficulty, and amenities of each. For 30 years, the guide has mapped out the wilderness areas of Isle Royale, but the current version is enhanced with color photos and downloadable maps. DuFresne details the park's flora, fauna, fishing opportunities, and history.

<<>>

L. David Mech, ***The Wolves of Isle Royale***, catalogs the author's study of wolves and moose on Isle Royale National Park based on his three-year research on the island. *Smithsonian Magazine* called Mech the world's foremost expert on wolves in the United States.

<<>>

Jeanne Meeks, ***Mystery on Isle Royale***, is the story of mother-daughter backpackers trying to strengthen their tattered relationship through a hiking experience. They find themselves enmeshed in mystery on the rugged island.

<<>>

Rolf Peterson, ***The Wolves of Isle Royale: A Broken Balance***, is a wildlife biologist's first-hand account of the relationship that exists between the wolves and the moose on the wilderness isle.

• Ghost Story

The Ghastly Demise of Charlie Mott. Hikers to Isle Royale, after hearing from a guide the tragic tale of Angelique and Charlie Mott, describe feeling a disquieting presence in secluded areas of the island. Whether Charlie has come back to spend time on the island that cost him his life, no one can say with certainty, but it is easy to understand the dissatisfaction he felt at his destiny.

In 1845 Angelique Mott was a seventeen-year-old Ojibwe woman, newly married to her French voyageur[4] husband Charlie. The couple joined a group of businessmen who hoped to get rich by discovering copper. In furtherance of that goal, they headed to Isle Royale.

---

[4]The term voyager came from the French word for traveler. They were eighteenth and nineteenth century French Canadians who engaged in transporting furs via canoe during the peak of the North American fur trade.

On the island, Angelique walked the beach and spotted a piece of mass copper shining from beneath the water and reported her findings to the businessmen. A deal was struck. Angelique and Charlie would stay on Isle Royale to guard the discovery, and supplies would be sent back to them within a fortnight. At the end of the summer, the men who hoped to have dealt with the business side of the venture would return to pick up the Motts.

Supplies never arrived. Angelique and Charlie lived on fish until a violent storm crashed in and destroyed their canoe. Soon their fishing nets were beyond repair. Each day they waited for their partners.

As winter set in, their food supply disappeared. They were starving. Still, no one came for them. They ate bark, roots, and bitter berries. Charlie traveled toward death faster than Angelique. He developed a fever and in delirium told Angelique he couldn't stand it anymore, and he was going to kill a sheep. He picked up a hunting knife and stared at his wife as he sharpened the tool. Angelique was horror-struck. She realized she was the sheep. She didn't dare take her eyes off Charlie for fear that the moment she did so, the knife would plunge into her heart. Fortunately, Charlie's senses returned before he carried out the deed.

By that time, Charlie was skin and bones. He slipped quietly into death. Angelique did not know what to do with the body since the ground was frozen. "It didn't seem right to just throw him out into the snow," she later recounted as she told the story. "If I kept him in the hut with me, the fire would rot his flesh."

Angelique left Charlie's corpse to freeze in the cabin and trudged off through the snow to build a lodge for herself. She feared hunger would tempt her to make a soup of Charlie. She believed it would be morally wrong, but she was afraid the same fever that had afflicted Charlie might strike her, making her take leave of her Christian values.

One day in front of her lean-to lodge, she saw rabbit tracks. She yanked hair from her head and wove it into a trap. She was so hungry that she ate raw meat from the first rabbit she caught. In a stroke of good fortune, miles down the beach from her camp, she found a deserted canoe, repaired it, and began fishing again.

One morning as she prepared her catch for breakfast, she heard a shot. The men who had promised to come for her were back, ten months late and likely assuming that both she and Charlie were dead. She ran toward the men.

"Where's Charlie?" they asked.

Angelique pointed toward the hut and replied, "He's asleep."

The men scurried off to locate Angelique's husband and secure his help in unloading their canoe. When they found the man dead, they removed his clothing to make sure Angelique hadn't murdered him, but it was apparent he had died of starvation.

Angelique returned to her mother in Sault Ste. Marie. She died in 1874. Hers was an amazing story of courage and perseverance.

It is unknown what became of Charlie's earthly remains, but some believe his spirit wanders Isle Royale and laments his misfortune.

20. Eagle Harbor
21. Eagle River

Eagle Harbor and **Eagle River**, eight miles apart, are along the route as you drive southwest on M-26 from the northernmost point of the Keweenaw Peninsula following the jagged edge of Lake Superior. Scenery and the Great Lake draw you to these two dots on the map.

The tiny hamlets provide views of the lake's hauntingly weathered coastline. A local pastime is watching freighters slip past the harbor, lakers if they sail the Great Lakes, and salties if they are ocean-going vessels.

Early voyagers named these villages for the many eagles they saw nesting along the banks. In the spring and fall, birders are entranced by 300 species of feathered friends. Eagles, falcons, vultures, owls, and more than 15 species of hawks have been spotted. Migrating birds fly over the Keweenaw Peninsula—north in the spring to their nesting areas and south in the fall to their winter homes.

Visitors from all over the U.S. arrive on the peninsula for the showy fall color tour. They mountain bike, hike, or drive the Brockway Mountain Drive that displays a panoply of jewel-toned reds, oranges, yellows, and purples. The route follows a nine-mile ridge of scenic roadway alongside M-26 between Eagle Harbor and Copper Harbor. It reaches elevations of 1,320 feet above sea level, the highest scenic roadway between the Rockies and the Alleghenies. The peak of the color tour is from the last week of September through the first two weeks of October which is slightly variable depending upon the year's weather.

Eagle Harbor, the northeastern of the two miniscule villages, lies nestled in its harbor of refuge facing the Great Lake. It is an unincorporated community that became a census-designated place in 2010. Its 2020 population was 100, down from its all-time high of 128 inhabitants in 2015. In its early days, this was an especially welcome harbor to sailors because it was midway between Sault Ste. Marie, Michigan, and Duluth, Minnesota, which made it the preferred spot for restocking supplies.

Eagle River is also a census-designated place and in 2020 boasted 70 inhabitants down from a 2010 population high of 71. The county seat of Keweenaw County, it is the least populated county seat in Michigan. Eagle River is eight miles southwest of Eagle Harbor along M-26.

Copper was a mainstay of the area economy by the mid-1800s. Eagle River, without a natural harbor like Eagle

Harbor, was important for its docks and warehouses built along the river for shipping the copper extracted from the nearby Cliff Mine. In a thirty-year span during the mid-1800s, investors shelled out $110,000 to get a piece of the copper action, and they earned a return of two million dollars on their money. Copper spawned other businesses and the area prospered.

• MUSEUMS

The **Eagle Harbor Schoolhouse**, corner of Third and Center Streets, was constructed in 1853. The one-room schoolhouse served the community until 1892 when it was deeded to the County Historical Society. The interior was furnished with period exhibits. It was designated a Michigan State Historic Site in 1971, and in 1972 was added to the National Register of Historic Places. It is open to the public seasonally.

Eagle Harbor School.
Courtesy of Pixabay Free Images.

<<>>

The **Eagle Harbor Lighthouse Maritime Museum** at the entrance to the Light Station grounds is owned by the Keweenaw County Historical Society. Exhibits include details of many Keweenaw shipwrecks and copper mining artifacts and memorabilia. The lighthouse compound also includes a 1927 Chrysler from the 1926 wreck of the *City of Bangor*. (See Shipwrecks Section.)

In 1999 Congress transferred ownership of the Eagle Harbor Light Station to the Historical Society. The Coast Guard continues to operate the light at the top of the tower.

Eagle Harbor Lighthouse Maritime Museum.
Courtesy of Bob Royce.

• Waterfalls, Parks, and Trails

Silver River Falls, on M-26 between Copper Harbor and Eagle Harbor. These beautiful waterfalls empty into a quiet creek with two sets of drops below a historic sandstone bridge. The upper drops are wide, and flow over conglomerate rock. The lower falls are more jagged. The steps to the waterfall are not handicap accessible, although if you can maneuver the stairs, it's an easy trail to the cascade.

• Another Stop to Consider

The Jampot, 6500 M-26, located in a brown wooden monastery on the Superior Coast, near Jacob's Falls, three mile east of Eagle River and five miles west of Eagle Harbor in Michigan's Keweenaw Peninsula. In 1986 this business sold its first jar of Poorrock Abbey™ preserves made from wild berries picked near the shop. Since that time, they have sold their wild berry preserves and other gourmet jams and jellies to customers from around the world. The line can be long, but customers insist it is worth the wait. As the years progressed, a variety of baked goods have been added to the available handmade delicacies. Seasonal and limited hours.

• LIGHTHOUSES

The **Eagle Harbor Light Station**, built in 1851, stands at the rocky entrance to the harbor and remains a working lighthouse, guiding sailors across the northern edge of the Keweenaw Peninsula.

Eagle Harbor Light Station.
Courtesy of Bob Royce.

The original lighthouse was replaced in 1871. The octagonal brick light tower is ten feet in diameter. Its walls are a foot thick, and the tower supports a 10-sided cast iron lantern. Lighthouse duties were performed by a head keeper and two assistant keepers. The light has undergone several changes over the years and was automated in 1980. It is filled with period furnishings and open to the public.

<<>>

Eagle River Light Station. On September 28, 1850, Congress appropriated $4,000 for a lighthouse "at or near the mouth of Eagle River." It took until January 1853 before land for the lighthouse was selected on the western side of the mouth of the Eagle River. The Eagle River Light was decommissioned in 1908, and the buildings sold at public auction.

• Shipwrecks

The ***City of Bangor*** and the ***Thomas Maytham*** were both lost during a late November storm in 1926. Initially, the Light Saving Station at Eagle Harbor was notified that the *Thomas Maytham*, carrying 20,000 tons of grain, was hung up on rocks 40 miles out in the lake. The rescue crew from the light station launched their motorboat, braced for the below-zero temperatures and thunderous waves, and headed to the site of the *Maytham*. They reached the ship and transferred the *Maytham*'s 22 crew members to their lifesaving vessel. During rescue efforts, the lifesaving station crew spotted a second ship, this one so covered with ice and snow that they could hardly tell it was a ship. This second ship was the *City of Bangor*, which had also run aground. The *Bangor* crew had made it to shore and were attempting to walk to Copper Harbor. The group had become lost and disoriented in the storm and in grave danger from the elements. The light station rescuers dropped off the crew of the *Maytham* and picked up the 29 men of the *City of Bangor*.

The *Bangor's* cargo was 248 new Chrysler automobiles. The cars were separated from the flooded engine room by a solid partition. Visual inspection showed they remained in good condition. The water around the wrecked ship froze solid, and an ice ramp was devised allowing the cars to be driven off the stranded vessel. Eventually, the cars were taken by train to Detroit, repaired, and sold.

The *City of Bangor* wreck site is now part of the Keweenaw Underwater Preserve and can be explored by divers. (See Underwater Preserve under Copper Harbor.)

• Book with a Tie to Eagle Harbor

M.C. Tillson and Lisa T. Bailey, ***The Mystery at Eagle Harbor (Michigan Lighthouse Adventure)***. Becky's and Sam's parents are researching Michigan lighthouses. Someone or something is following them, and they encounter more questions than answers as they grow determined to solve the mysteries of Eagle Harbor and the ghost who has been haunting the lighthouse for 100 years.

• Ghost Story

The Ghost of the Eagle Harbor Lighthouse. The Coast Guard lighthouse keeper in the 1970s reported many strange occurrences at the Eagle Harbor Lighthouse. A faceless man wearing a plaid flannel shirt wandered the premises. The keeper heard the sounds of moving furniture and heavy footsteps coming from the second-floor bedroom. Lights flitted on and off. The keeper also reported seeing light coming from under the door to the tower. If he opened the door to look, the light disappeared until he closed the door, and then the glow could again be seen in the tiny slit beneath the door's threshold. Sometimes the keeper's alarm clock would be moved or turned off.

So disconcerting were these occurrences that the unnerved man asked for a transfer citing the lighthouse's haunting as his reason. His request was ignored. After another year passed, the keeper claimed the haunting grew worse. He was awakened in the middle of the night—especially in winter—by voices and footsteps. Perhaps the explanation for the disquieting events lies buried in the pages of the book written about the haunting. (See Book with a Tie to Eagle Harbor.)

22. Ontonagon

The Village of Ontonagon, located along the south shore of Lake Superior in the western Upper Peninsula, had a 2020 population of 1,242. Founded in 1843, Ontonagon sits at the mouth of the Ontonagon River which gives its name to both the village and the county. The river is the largest that flows into the south shores of Lake Superior.

Ontonagon is the only city/village/town in the world with that name. There is more than one theory about the derivation of the name. In the Ojibwe language, the word *Nondon-organ* means hunting river. A French transliteration called it the River Nanton Nagunon on a map published in 1672.

The second theory comes with a story. The Ojibwe word *onagon* means dish or bowl. *Nintonaganing* means the place of my dish. Bishop Baraga wrote that, according to legend, an Ojibwe woman was washing her dish in the river and dropped it. The river carried the dish away, and she exclaimed, "*Nia! Nind Onagon*!" which translated, "Oh! My dish! My dish!" Supposedly the river became known to the Ojibwe as the River of the Lost Bowl.

Rugged adventurers love the region around Ontonagon for its superb hiking, biking, backpacking, fishing, hunting, snowshoeing, cross-country skiing, canoeing, kayaking, and sledding that awaits them and makes every season memorable. The Porcupine Mountains Wilderness State Park offers limitless exploration, and there are more than 100 waterfalls in the area including Agate Falls, Bond Falls, Cascade Falls, Greenstone Falls, Greenwood Falls, Nonesuch Falls, O-Kun-de-Kun Falls, and Overlooked Falls.

A 1½ ton copper mass known as the Ontonagon Boulder is credited with starting the copper boom in the U.P. The Ojibwe had long known about the copper megalith and treated it as a shrine to their Manitou, a mediator between them and the Great Spirit. The enormous rock lay on the west branch of the Ontonagon River, near the present-day location of the Victoria Hydroelectric Dam. Several early explorers to the region tried to move the immense rock. None was successful, although many took small pieces as souvenirs. The boulder was sent to the Smithsonian Museum of Natural History in 1843 and remains on display there in Washington, D.C.

• Museum

Ontonagon County Historical Society Museum, 422 River Street, contains exhibits of the county's history of mining, logging, farming, and maritime heritage. There is also a gift shop. The museum is the starting point for lighthouse tours available three times a day in the summer. The museum is seasonal with limited hours.

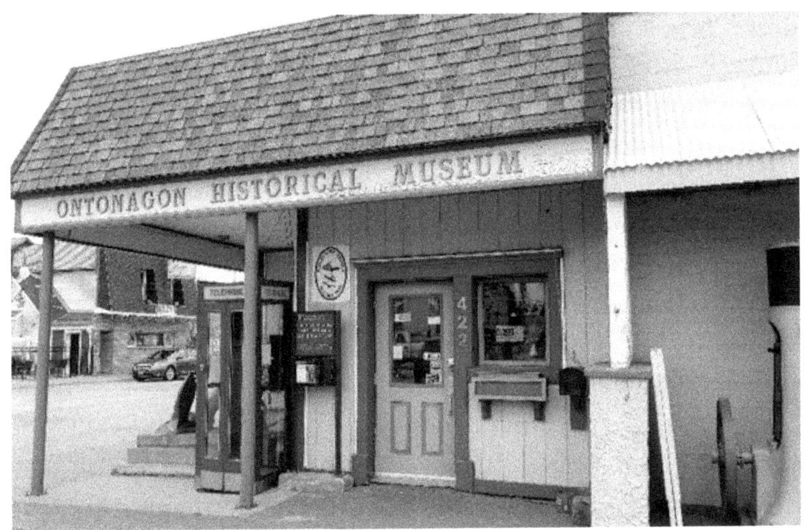

Ontonagon Historical Museum.
Courtesy of Bob Royce.

• Beaches, Parks, and Trails

Bond Falls is a scenic waterfall in southern Ontonagon County. The falls come from the middle branch of the Ontonagon River as it tumbles over a thick slab of fractured rock, dividing it into many small cascades. The falls drop about 50 feet. An accessible boardwalk offers six viewing locations.

<<>>

The **Porcupine Mountains Wilderness State Park** with 60,000 acres is Michigan's largest state park. Old-growth forests cover 35,000 acres. The park is home to roaring waterfalls, miles of rivers, streams, and Lake Superior shoreline. More than 90 miles of hiking trails open to vistas of unsurpassed beauty. **Lake of the Clouds** and **Summit Peak** are both located in the park. Lake of the Clouds is the most photographed spot in the park.

From the Lake of the Clouds parking lot, you can take **Big Carp River Trail** to the top of the ridge for an amazing view of the lake before you descend into the forest. Summit Peak is the highest point in the park, nearly 2,000 feet above sea level, with a 50-foot viewing tower, it is easily reached after a short hike. The **Lake Superior Trail** runs along the northern edge of the park for ten miles of rugged, secluded terrain that rewards the hardy hiker with spectacular views. **Union Bay Beaches**, along a two-mile stretch of shoreline on the eastern end of Porcupine Mountains Wilderness State Park, offer accessible sandy beaches that are perfect for swimming (if you don't mind cold water) and agate hunting. The beaches are accessible from several points on M-10.

• Lighthouses

The **Ontonagon Harbor Lighthouse**, constructed in 1866 to replace the original wooden structure built in 1851 and 1852, is owned by the Ontonagon County Historical Society. The Historical Society offers tours that start from the museum site, 422 River Street. The Ontonagon Lighthouse contains period furnishings obtained by the Historical Society to show visitors what Ontonagon was like in the early 1900s. The copper and lumber booms brought ships into the Ontonagon Harbor and necessitated a lighthouse to increase safety.

The lighthouse was built schoolhouse-style, similar to Sand Point Lighthouses in Escanaba and Copper Harbor. A frequent question asked of the tour guides is, "Why isn't the lighthouse right on the shoreline?" The answer is that originally it was. It had a high basement to protect it from monster waves, but deposits of sediment have increased the width of the land strip between the lighthouse and water.

The lighthouse was deactivated in 1963 when an automatic foghorn was installed on the west pier, and a battery light was located at the end of the east pier providing safer entrance into the Ontonagon Harbor. The light is still lit, however, and guides pleasure craft into the harbor. The lighthouse was added to the National Register of Historic Places in 1975.

<<>>

Ontonagon West Pierhead Lighthouse. The Ontonagon River is wide, but a bar at its mouth prevented ships from turning into the river for shelter. When copper mining started near Ontonagon in 1848, vessels that brought in supplies and carried away the prized copper had to anchor offshore and load and unload with the aid of lighters.[5]

In 1851 the first piers at the mouth of the river were constructed. They were a means of extending the harbor out into the lake. Built of wood, they were no match for Superior's wrathful storms. Charles Harvey, who was finishing work on the Soo Canal Locks in 1855, was solicited by the mining companies to build stout locks at the Ontonagon River's entrance in return for a percentage of the copper profits. Harvey's pier was also a failure.

It was time to bring in the federal government which from 1889-1908 tackled the slow project of constructing on parallel piers. The Ontonagon Lighthouse had been given responsibility for the pierhead beacon established on the west side of the river's mouth in 1853. In 1889 an iron gallery was placed around the pierhead light to enable the keeper to clean the lantern room glass, and four ventilators were installed in the lantern's parapet. James Corgan served as keeper of the main and pierhead light in 1910.

---

[5] A lighter is a flat-bottomed barge used by moored ships to transfer goods and passengers.

He reached the pierhead tower by following a 750-foot-long boardwalk from the main lighthouse to the pier, walking 600 feet on the pier, and then taking the 1,200-foot-long elevated walkway to the tower.

• Ghost Stories

The Ontonagon Triangle is an area where at least four people disappeared under suspicious circumstances. All went missing within a 50-square-mile area between Ontonagon and Houghton counties. The remains of only one of the four have ever been found, and those were discovered years after the man vanished. Although none of the four seems to have returned to haunt the area, the disappearances in the Ontonagon Triangle have taken place under circumstances allegedly involving the paranormal.

John Buccanero was 22 years old when he disappeared. He was last seen riding a snowmobile in 1987. More than 200 searchers attempted to find him. Months after he went missing, loggers spotted his deserted snowmobile in another part of the forest from where he went missing. The snowmobile didn't help the searchers locate the missing man. A human skull was found 15 years after Buccanero's disappearance. Alongside the head were a snowmobile suit and a helmet. Dental records confirmed it was Buccanero. He is the only one of the four missing persons whose remains have been found.

On November 16, 1988, Oscar Hintta, 64, vanished while hunting with his best friend. Hintta was a retired custodian from Calumet. The buddies went off in different directions, and Hintta was never seen again. Hundreds of searchers, some using aircraft and dogs, turned up no trace of the missing man.

Raymond Lewis, a 55-year-old poet and handyman from Dollar Bay, disappeared on a forest road in 1992. His truck turned up a short distance from where John Buccanero had disappeared seven years earlier.

In August 1993, Jan Pattison, 38, vanished into the dense forest, never to be seen again. The evening of her disappearance, she met two elderly men and accompanied them to their cabin. The trio was drinking. At 10:30 p.m., Pattison left the cabin. She never arrived home. Her 1981 Ford Tempo 300 was found a month later just off a two-track dirt trail. Her personal belongings—keys, purse, cigarettes—were inside the car. Extensive searches covered the area, but her whereabouts remain a mystery. The two men who had last been with Pattison were ruled out as suspects. The police found footprints that emerged from a creek near the abandoned car. The prints continued for three or four miles along an old logging trail before disappearing onto a gravel road. Police took casts of a woman's size-7 footprints. The casts suggested shoes similar to the nurse's shoes that Pattison usually wore. Dogs were unable to follow the missing woman's scent.

People go missing. What makes these cases stranger than the normal missing persons case is that their vehicles were found, but there were no signs of foul play, and it would seem that with extensive searches, the bodies should have shown up. Other than Buccanero, there's no trace of the missing people.

<<>>

The Ghost of the Paulding Light, 13½ miles southeast of Ontonagon. The light is visible from Robbins Pond Road, also known as Old State 45. The most popular viewing area is along a guardrail barricading Robbins Pond Road to through traffic. The light, sometimes called the Dog Meadow Light, has remained a mystery in the Upper Peninsula for more than a century.

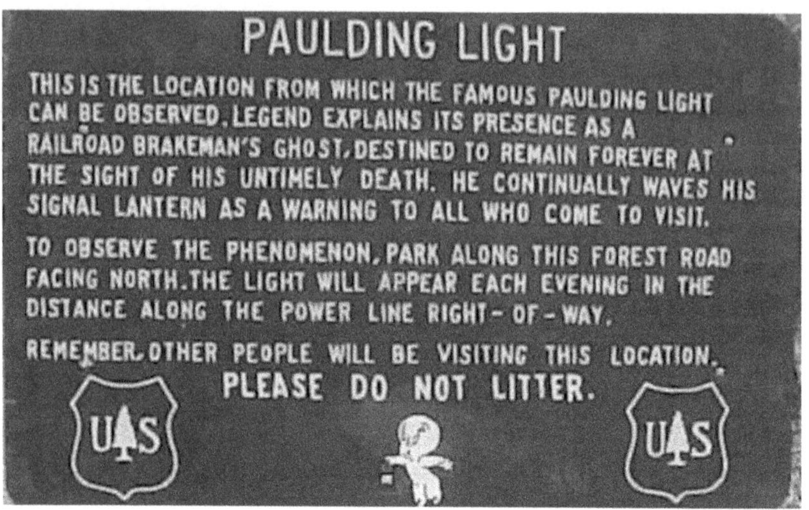

Signs, like the one on the one above, are posted by the Forest Service of the U.S. Department of Agriculture marking the best spots from which to observe the lights. The signs also provide a purported explanation for the phenomenon.

An alternate story suggests a child went missing one night after darkness had fallen. The little boy's father grabbed a lantern and went looking for his son. The man was hit by a train and his ghost continues its search.

Ripley's Believe It or Not offered more than $100,000 to the person or persons who could solve the mystery.

<<>>

There are rumors of a young woman who died of diphtheria in the Ontonagon Lighthouse in 1885 coming back to haunt the light. No details have been found to corroborate or embellish the story.

23. Silver City

Silver City is noted by the census authorities to be a populated place without statistics. Barely even a village, but possessing the audacity to call itself a city, the hamlet lies at the junction of Highways M-64 and M-107 on the shore of Lake Superior at the mouth of the Iron River. Silver City was founded in the late 1870s and took its name from the small vein of silver discovered just south of the village. The resultant silver rush was short-lived since not enough of the precious metal was found to make mining profitable.

The tiny burg stakes its claim to fame as the **Gateway to the Porcupine Mountains**. (See Ontonagon for additional information about the Porcupine Mountain Wilderness State Park and activities in the area.)

The Porcupine Mountains, or Porkies, are a group of small mountains spanning the northwestern Upper Peninsula of Michigan in Ontonagon and Gogebic counties. They were named by the native Ojibwe who, according to legend, thought the silhouette of the mountains was shaped like a porcupine.

• A Park

Green Park, Green Park Road between Silver City and Ontonagon on the shoreline. An easy to miss park with a sandy beach that includes a rocky vein perfect for your agate search.

• Other Stops to Consider

Bonanza Falls, located on the Big Iron River. From Silver City, take M-64 south and follow the highway signage to Bonanza Falls via a short gravel road on the west side of the highway. The falls cascade in small incremental drops that accumulate in natural pools. They may not cause you to gasp in awe but are a relaxing spot to spend a warm summer afternoon.

<<>>

Carp Lake Mine, M-107, west of Silver City. The Carp Lake Mining Company was organized in 1858, and mining activity began the next year. During its active years, the Carp Lake Mine produced approximately 34,000 pounds of copper. Visitors can explore the mine and may find copper on rock piles. However, State Parks do not allow collecting or removal.

<<>>

Porcupine Mountains Ski Area, M-64, offers a small local ski hill. This is not Vail or Aspen and may seem a bit out of the way. The lift is slow, and the hill isn't usually crowded. But the views of Lake Superior are, well, superior. The scenery is probably the most magnificent during the fall color tour when taking the lift (minus snow) to look down on the blaze-colored forest to the lake may make this a stop you'll always remember.

Overland to the Northern Shore of Lake Michigan

This travel guide focuses on Michigan's coastlines that are part of the St. Lawrence Seaway. At this point, it has covered Michigan's Lake Superior cities, towns, and villages. You can backtrack around the Upper Peninsula and stay alongside the water like the huge freighters navigate.

Or you can go overland and pick up your journey at Menominee along northwest Lake Michigan bordering the southern coast of Michigan's Upper Peninsula.

This route will take about 3½ hours, and you'll pass through Crystal Falls where you may want to stop and stretch your legs at Bewabic park on the shore of Fortune Lake.

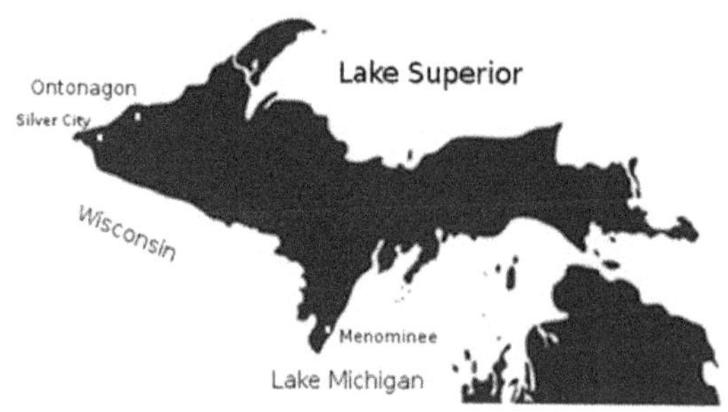

LAKE MICHIGAN

The northern coast of Lake Michigan hugs the southern shore of Michigan's Upper Peninsula. In 1634 French cartographer, Nicholas Sanson, published a map of North America that included the Great Lakes. Lake Michigan was identified for the first time and was labeled "Lac de Puans," which means Lake of the Stinking Things. The name derives from the appellation "stinking people" given to the local Winnebago tribe. It was no reflection upon the Winnebago's hygiene; rather a reference to their migration from land near the ocean (stinking or saltwater). Fortunately, that original name did not stick. The legend of the tribe coming from a place of stinking water fueled the belief held by the French that if they pushed far enough west, they would reach the other stinking ocean and the waterway to China.

Even without written documentation of its earliest history, Lake Michigan left its story etched in the rocks, sand, gorges, falls, dunes, and beaches around its shores. Three billion years ago, during the Precambrian Era, the world was a place of enormous volcanic activity. Earth-shaking movement gave rise to the embryonic stage of Lake Michigan. Birth was a long, drawn-out process. Not until more recently, a mere 600 million years ago when the Paleozoic Era arrived, did water become an important part of the development process.

During the Paleozoic Era, the Great Lakes region was flooded by ancient marine seas that contained the area's first life forms: corals, crinoids, mollusks, and brachiopods. The early seas also left lime, clay, salt, and sand which eventually became the limestone, shale, sandstone, halite, and gypsum that is mined today.

The Pleistocene Epoch, the time era before the modern era, was known as the Great Ice Age. It began about a million years ago and lasted until 10,000 years ago. This was the time of gargantuan glaciers, up to 6,500 feet thick, that steadily inched their way over the Great Lakes region. As the glaciers receded, huge amounts of water melted, creating glacier lakes much larger than the Great Lakes we currently know. In a phenomenon called uplift, the land began to rise. This process continues today and means that Lake Michigan and the other four lakes will continue to see changes by a process so slow that to human experience it is imperceptible.

Then came man. About 10,000 to 14,000 years ago at the end of the Great Ice Age, there is evidence of prehistoric Paleo-Indian culture existing in North America. The prevailing theory suggests the first humans in North America traveled over a now extinct Siberian land bridge. Other theories continue to be explored, but the land bridge theory is based, at least in part, on the lack of evidence of earlier pre-humans on the continent.

The Paleo-Indian culture is marked by big-game hunting and the development of simple tools. Kill sites have been identified with evidence of distinctive spearheads made of fluted chipped stones. With these elemental spears, called Clovis stones, hunters stalked great mastodon, mammoth, and bison.

Nearly 7,000 years ago, early inhabitants discovered copper and began using it for hunting, in religious practices, and for ornamentation. These early humans developed agriculture and refined their method of killing game.

The earliest known beings of the Great Lakes Region of North America are the Anishinaabe who are the forebears of the Ojibwe and other Algonquin speaking tribes of the Great Lakes. They maintained a rich oral history passed from generation to generation over centuries, tracking important events and religious practices. Unfortunately, the written history of the Great Lakes original people is sketchy. Although early French, Dutch, and English explorers kept detailed journals beginning in the 1500s, they wrote from a European perspective, subject to cultural and language differences, and therefore much was lost in translation. The Anishinaabe oral history suggests they came from land near the Atlantic Ocean.

According to prevailing legend, a prophet to the Anishinaabe warned his people "if you do not move, you will be destroyed." The Anishinaabe listened to the messenger and left their villages along the Atlantic seashore. They embarked on an epic westward journey in search of a new home. The Anishinaabe were guided by signs from the spirits that led them to a bountiful country where food was plentiful, and they could avoid the prophesied disaster which some believe may have been a forewarning that Europeans were coming.

The Anishinaabe's courageous trek lasted for many generations and took them through the entire Great Lakes region, down the St. Lawrence River, and eventually overland through the heart of Michigan to the east side of Lake Michigan and around the whole of Lake Superior.

The Anishinaabe broke into three groups. The Pottawatomie (Bodawatamie) settled along the Lake Michigan shoreline where the abundant water provided them with food and waterways for travel. In southwestern Michigan, they hunted the plentiful game and raised crops. The Pottawatomie pledged to safeguard the sacred fire for the Anishinaabe.

A second group became known as the Odawa (Ottawa). They remained in the area of the upper part of the lower peninsula of Michigan and on Manitoulin Island. They agreed to carry out major trading expeditions for their people.

The third group became known as the Ojibwe (Also spelled Ojibwa and Chippewa). They settled in the Upper Peninsula of Michigan, Minnesota, and Wisconsin. The role of the Ojibwe was to protect the spiritual beliefs of the Anishinaabe and from their numbers came the Midewiwin, or religious leader, who would preserve the sacred lore of the people in words and songs and symbols they inscribed on birchbark scrolls.

The story of the Anishinaabe became inextricably entwined with the story of the Europeans who began arriving in Michigan in the 1500s. From the landing of Christopher Columbus in 1492, the New World and the possibility of a trade route to China by way of a Northwest Passage captured the minds of zealous explorers who believed they would be the lucky ones to find it. They pleaded their cases to ruling monarchs, besieging them for authority to sail and for provisions to sustain them on their journey.

The first European to explore and map the St. Lawrence area was Sea Captain Jacques Cartier, born in St. Malo, France, in 1491. In 1534 French King Frances I approved Cartier's travel to North America in search of gold or other riches and, more importantly, a passage to Cathay or China. Cartier never made it into the Great Lakes, but his was the first documented exploration of inland North America. He interacted with the Original People (Iroquois and Micmac Nations) in the area near present day Quebec. The Native People regaled him with tales of wealthy kingdoms further up the river. Cartier boldly annexed the St. Lawrence River Valley to the Crown of France.

Samuel de Champlain was a young man when his visionary king, Henry IV, granted him permission to sail to New France. He was the first European to see the Great Lakes. In 1615 he sailed into the top of Lake Huron, naming it the Great Sweetwater Sea. Of the five lakes, Huron was the first discovered, Michigan the last. Not an arrogant man, Champlain considered himself a geographer, although he was a soldier, explorer, anthropologist, artist, author, naturalist, and cartographer. He was also a profuse writer and drew maps to help future explorers. In one of his early maps, Champlain depicted all of the Great Lakes except Michigan. In some respects, the map was accurate, and his skill with navigational instruments and his dedication to accuracy (as far as he could determine it), made his maps the most respected Great Lakes maps of his time.

In 1634 Champlain sent his loyal follower, Jean Nicolet, to further explore the Great Lakes. Again, the motivation was to find the Northwest Passage, but instead Nicolet found the final of the five Great Lakes. Nicolet did not explore the entire lake and Nicholas Sanson's resulting map of 1634, based upon Jean Nicolet's explorations, presents a truncated and badly distorted Lake Michigan.

The late 1600s and early 1700s were the periods of the Jesuits. As eager as explorers were to find new lands, missionaries like Father Jacques Marquette were equally enthusiastic about converting the Anishinaabe to Christianity. In 1670 as a result of their missionizing and exploring in the area, Father Marquette and Louis Joliet discovered the true, elongated shape of the fifth lake. They changed its name from the ignoble, "Lake of Stinking Things" to Lake Michigan. The name-game was far from over. A map from 1675 labeled Lake Michigan, Lac St. Joseph, and another French explorer called it *Lac Daupin* in honor of the king's son. Jesuit Father Hennepin described it as Michigonong, and local Native Americans called it Michigami. Ultimately, Lake Michigan stuck.

Father Marquette founded the village of St. Ignace, and it is at his mission there that his bones lie today. He died on the shore of Lake Michigan near Ludington (or some say Frankfort or Cross Village), and Native Americans cleaned his bones according to their custom, then carried them back to his mission, and deposited them in a coffin of birch bark in a consecrated spot. Father Marquette allegedly died of exhaustion after a long and difficult exploration, but the best that can be said with some certainty is that he died of natural causes.

Although other Jesuits who explored the Great Lakes brought the words of their God to the Native Americans, none is as well-remembered as Father Marquette. Cities, rivers, streets, and churches are named in his honor and perpetuate his memory.

The Original People of Lake Michigan's Coast had an abiding respect for the land. The culture with which they imbued the area made it rich in heritage.

Europeans were lured to the Upper Peninsula by fur-bearing animals. (See Lake Michigan in Book Three. *Exploring Michigan's Sunset Coasts* for additional discussion of the fur trade.)

Lake Michigan shores became a melting pot. Europeans from more than twenty nations came in large numbers. They endured life-threatening, and often life-ending, hardships. They left behind loved ones and crossed the Atlantic. Some, like the Irish, were wretchedly poor and came to escape extreme poverty or outright starvation. Others, like the Germans, Dutch, Finns, and Swedes came to escape political turmoil. Others, like the Danes, Poles, Italians, and Norwegians came to create a new life. Germans came in the highest numbers. They were actively recruited by the State of Michigan, which published and sent a guide to the Commissioner of Immigration, E. H. Thompson, in Germany during years of revolution. The book urged Germans, who needed little convincing, to buy Michigan land. They settled everywhere there was fertile soil and began farming. Many Norwegians settled in the port towns of Lake Michigan and resumed the work they knew—shipbuilding.

Lake Michigan fur trading, lumbering, and farming all took a turn as the mainstay of Lake Michigan's shoreline economy. But fishing predated those industries, coexisted while each reigned supreme, outlasted them, and continues today as a source of income to the commercial fisheries and a source of joy to the sport fishers who will tell you there is nothing like a day spent angling.

History cannot date the first Native American's fishing attempt, but it's certain it did not take long for the Anishinaabe to discover the Great Lakes' wealth of fish. Commercial fishing experienced a growth spurt in the early 1800s and by 1848, Lake Michigan fishing was an important source of food and income. The lake brimmed with trout, herring, whitefish, yellow perch, shiners, suckers, and seven species of chub. These fish had evolved collectively to develop a balanced and mutually compatible system that began with the retreat of the glaciers. Key to the success of this ecosystem was Niagara Falls, which served as a natural barrier to fish and other organisms coming from the Atlantic. The Falls prevented outside species from entering the Great Lakes and disrupting the Lakes' delicate balance.

In the mid-1800s, Michigan's annual catch increased by nearly 20% per year until 1889 when the fishing industry produced a record 147 million pounds of fish. During the next 60 years, the fishing methods improved, but the annual catch declined so that by the mid-1900s, it was down 25 percent from its heyday.

Pollution of the lakes was a major factor in the decline of the fish population. Lumbering led to soil erosion, and topsoil washed into the rivers and streams that fed into the lakes. Pulp and paper mills caused chemical pollution and dumped sawdust into the lakes. The sawdust rotted and used up oxygen.

Mercury, used in the paper industry, was likely the most dangerous contaminant introduced into the lakes. Eventually, mercury was banned in the production of paper, but it still found its way into the water because of contamination from power plants burning mercury-rich coal. Consumers worried about the mercury content of fish caught in the lakes. In 2002 every state bordering a Great Lake issued an advisory warning about the health dangers of consuming Great Lakes fish.

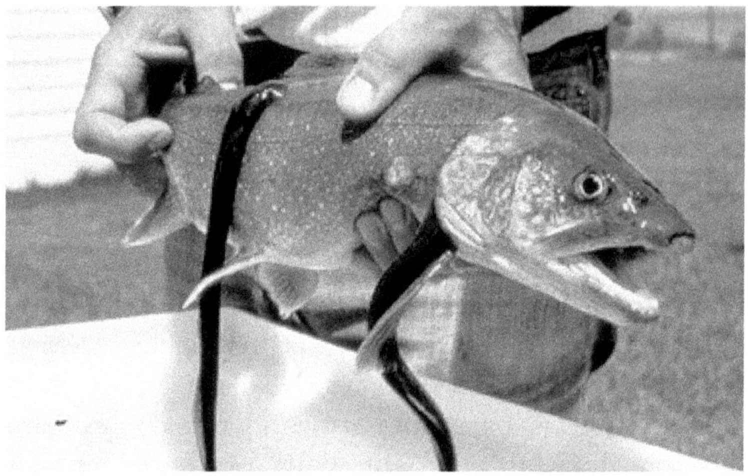

Sea Lamprey attached to Lake Trout.
Courtesy of Pixabay Free Images.

By 1850 there were more than a million Americans and Canadians living in the Great Lakes basin. Farming was a major industry, and it exacerbated the serious erosion problem affecting the lakes. A century later, by the mid-1900s, the problem was dramatically compounded by the addition of pesticides and fertilizer to crops. The fertilizers washed into the lakes and increased the growth of water plants, including algae. The decay of these plants, like the rotting of the sawdust dumped by mills, depleted the lakes of vital oxygen and in turn killed great numbers of fish.

The pollution of the Great Lakes increased significantly with the rise of large cities like Chicago, Milwaukee, and Detroit. Large industries covered shorelines along the Great Lakes waterways exacerbating the pollution problem.

Congress passed the Federal Clean Water Act in 1972. It marked the turning point for Great Lakes water quality improvement.

Unfortunately, it hasn't been steady improvement. New contaminants including coal ash create problems. Climate change affects water quality. Some lakeside cities limp along with inadequate sewer systems dumping billions of gallons of sewage into the lakes annually. Work is far from finished on cleaning up the Great Lakes and keeping them clean.

An old Cree provide warns, "Only when the last tree has died and the last river has been poisoned and the last fish been caught will we realize we cannot eat money."

Shipwrecks of Lake Michigan

Say that 'I loved old ships,'
write nothing more upon my tombstone,
and they who read it will know
that I loved the roar of the breakers
in bygone sailing days.
-W. H. Van Dyke

Ocean sailors speak of Great Lakes sailors with derision. The latter are not real sailors. They do not face the challenge of the mighty saltwater oceans with their tides, unpredictability, and sudden storms. And the lake sailor has the shore and escape nearby.

But ridicule evaporates the first time an ocean sailor confronts the tempestuous wrath of these great inland seas. Caught in a freshwater hurricane, they swear "never again" to sailing the Sweetwater Seas. Lake Michigan has singlehandedly claimed 800 ships, slightly more than 20 percent of the ships that have gone down on the Lakes.

In November, when winter is threatening, but fall has not quite given up the fight, sailors play Russian Roulette to complete a last trip of the season. They push the limits. They ignore the warnings. And sometimes they pay with their lives.

The ship disasters described below belong to Lake Michigan, although many went down closer to the Wisconsin shore. The Great Lake knows no boundaries and chooses her victims with caprice. The five are among the more compelling. Additional calamities are noted under the city where the ship rests.

The ***Phoenix*** sank on November 21, 1847. In medieval times the mythical phoenix was common in Egyptian, Asian, and Greek culture. When the eagle-sized phoenix grew old, it made a nest and set it on fire. The flames consumed the bird which was then reborn from the ashes.

In a stroke of macabre irony, the steamer *Phoenix*, named for that mythical bird, was one of the first vessels to burn on the Great Lakes, but nothing rose from her smoldering ashes. At the time of her demise, the *Phoenix* was still in her infancy, a mere two years old.

Almost all westbound travel in those days was by boat through the Great Lakes. The wave of immigration headed westward caused ships to stretch their capacity. On her final voyage of the season, the *Phoenix* was packed to bursting with about seventy Americans and more than two hundred Dutch immigrants. Only a handful of the latter had cabins. The remaining passengers crowded in steerage or found space on deck. Even the cargo hold was filled to bursting. The crew of 29 looked forward to this last trip of the season, but their anticipation was tempered by the knowledge that late November voyages were fraught with danger.

The *Phoenix* left Buffalo on November 11. On the 13th, she was still in Lake Erie. A week later, on Saturday, November 20, the *Phoenix* arrived in Manitowoc, Wisconsin, with her cargo of coffee, molasses, sugar, and hardware destined for that port. Ugly weather forced her to remain in harbor for several hours after the cargo was removed. About 1:00 a.m. on November 21, Captain Sweet gave the order to continue the voyage that was intended to end at Chicago. He expected to make the next port of his journey by daylight.

It was about 4:00 a.m. when flames were noticed over the boiler on the underside of the deck. About the same time, flames sprouted from the ventilators that moved hot air from the boiler room. Crew members, with the assistance of some passengers, immediately started fighting the blaze. Bucket brigades were set up, but the fire had a good start and raged out of control in spite of the efforts.

The ship was doomed. Passengers continued trying to extinguish the flames; others threw themselves into the water. The two lifeboats on board were launched. Captain Sweet manned one and his first mate the other. They intended to ferry people back and forth from the burning ship to shore. The lifeboats together could accommodate slightly less than 50 passengers at a time. The fire spread so quickly that there would never be a second trip. Shrieks of terror sang to a backdrop of crackling fire and a softer chorus of unanswered prayers.

The passengers still aboard, and deserted by their captain, had to choose between the devil and the deep blue sea—remain on board and burn or jump overboard to a certain death in the frigid waters. The Hazelton sisters, returning from school in the East, jumped. They clasped each other in a tight embrace and leapt to their deaths almost within sight of their home harbor. A young mother hugged her wailing infant close to her body and dropped from the burning deck into the restless waters that claimed them both. Family members kissed and hugged one last time before plunging to their death in the waiting waves.

Other ships hovered in the area and rushed to offer assistance to the blazing *Phoenix*. The *Delaware*, first to arrive, found only three survivors: three crewmen who clung tenuously to the rudder chains of the charred hull. Everyone else was dead. Lake Michigan was littered with bodies. The final death toll was estimated at 258, most of whom were Dutch immigrants.

The high casualty rate was attributed to the lack of sufficient lifeboats, but the cause of the fire would be blamed on the Second Engineer who allowed the boilers to overheat. Why he did not properly monitor the boilers is the subject of much speculation. Perhaps he fell asleep.

Perhaps he imbibed in a few too many drinks when they were delayed in Manitowoc that afternoon. Perhaps he had stepped away from his post for an unknown reason. Whatever caused him to shirk his duty, the ship was lost.

<<>>

The ***Niagara*** went down on September 24, 1856. She was built in 1846, and during her decade of sailing, she earned a legacy that would endure after her demise. She brought thousands of German and Scandinavian immigrants from Canada and New York to start new lives in Wisconsin and Michigan. She was one of the strongest and most powerful ships built in the mid-1800s. As her strength sapped the night she sank, she witnessed heroism; she witnessed evil; and she witnessed rank, unmitigated terror.

The *Niagara* left Sheboygan, Wisconsin, bound for Chicago with 100 cabin and nearly 200 steerage passengers aboard. Captain Fred S. Miller, expecting a calm and uneventful trip, grabbed a quick afternoon nap. He was awakened by screams of "Fire!" A cloud of black smoke and blazing flames rose from the engine room. Captain Miller wasted no time getting the fire hose in position, and the engineer began to douse the flames. The captain rushed to the pilothouse and ordered the ship turned toward shore. Within a few minutes, the engine had stopped, and the burning ship foundered—safety a short distance away.

It was not uncommon in the mid-1800s for a ship to lack life preservers, so the frantic Captain assisted by several passengers, began pulling down stateroom doors and pitching them into the lake along with gangplanks, chairs, washstands, and anything else that looked likely to float. They had only a few minutes to accomplish these last-ditch efforts before the center portion of the boat was engulfed in fire. Most of the crew was trapped forward with no movement possible between the stern and the bow.

Mishaps with lifeboats may have been the single largest cause of death from the disaster. Fear-crazed passengers attempted to launch lifeboats on their own. The largest of the lifeboats capsized upon hitting water.

Acts of courage and cowardice commingled that night. One lifeboat, safely lowered into the water with women and children aboard, was rushed by a group of men who jumped into it from the deck above. The flimsy lifeboat flipped, sending all but four of its occupants to the depths of Lake Michigan.

An even more despicable act of cowardice was attributed to former Wisconsin congressman, John B. Macy who in his better days was described as a brave man with a cool head. Perhaps the scenes he witnessed that night addled his normally clear brain. Macy, a rather portly gentleman who could not swim, is said to have screamed, "Oh, God, someone save me. Ten thousand—a hundred thousand to the man who will save my life." Getting no takers, he spotted a lifeboat filled with women and children being lowered into the water; one end was lower than the other. He jumped, and his prodigious weight caused the ropes to break, casting everyone inside the unbalanced life craft to a watery grave. The ex-congressman was never seen again.

Standing at the railing next to Macy, when the congressman made his ignoble offer of reward, was a tiny lad maybe two years old. His parents were nowhere in sight. A deckhand ignored Macy's pleas but picked up the child and jumped into the water clutching the toddler tightly. The deckhand grabbed a piece of floating gangplank and courageously paddled them toward shore. By the next morning, the two were found where they had drifted onto the beach. Both lived, but the deckhand left town, and his name was never known. He remains the anonymous hero of the tragedy.

The child was taken in by a couple in the area and identified as Frank Willette, the name on a small gold cross that hung from his neck. His new caretakers advertised in newspapers throughout the country, but no one claimed the child. Several decades passed and the young man, who went by the name of Frank Willis, made his own attempt to locate family by running ads similar to those run many years earlier. Defying all odds, he was contacted by an aunt residing in Nebraska and a cousin in Manitowoc. They confirmed his real name was Frank Willette as had been engraved on his cross. His parents, a brother, and a sister had died in the *Niagara* tragedy.

On the evening of September 24th, with safety only a mile or so away, and beaches clearly in sight of those slipping under water for the last time, at least 150 either drowned or burned. If that is not a sad enough ending to this story, there was also speculation that the fire was intentionally set.

On a previous trip, just after the ship left port, a steward found a note on the table in his room: "Look out. Save yourself. The boat will be burned tonight. Everything is in readiness." Had a crazy person sent the note and then lacked the courage to carry out the threat until the next trip? Some questions will never be answered.

<<>>

The ***Lady Elgin*** slipped beneath the water on September 7, 1860. All ships lost, sunk, or missing are cloaked in sadness, loss, and despair. Some engender rage or anger when it is revealed that human carelessness or stupidity like the stories of the *Phoenix* and the *Niagara* above played a significant role. Other catastrophes could not have been avoided. A few capture our imaginations like the Christmas Tree Ship because of the cargo she carried or the human circumstances surrounding her last voyage. But there is no other ship that carries the overtones of intrigue, espionage, or possible sabotage like the *Lady Elgin*.

The *Lady Elgin* was a monster-sized, side-wheeled steamer 252 feet in length. She boasted more than a thousand-ton displacement. She was one of the largest vessels afloat on the Great Lakes in the mid-1800s. She was built to honor the wife of the Governor General of Canada, Lord Elgin.

The *Lady* had her detractors. They charged she was cursed from the day of her launch in 1851. Her boilers and engine had been salvaged from the *Cleopatra*, an ocean slave trader ship that was confiscated by the U.S. Navy. The *Cleopatra* was steeped in grim stories of human beings torn from their homelands and sold as chattel in a strange land. Perhaps the evil that shrouded the *Cleopatra* marked the *Lady Elgin* because she used those tainted parts.

When the *Lady* went down, stories hinted, or in some cases boldly asserted, she was rammed intentionally by the schooner *Augusta* which was sent to destroy her. The slavery issue, some argued, was entwined a second time with the *Lady Elgin*, and a reckoning was demanded. A number of southern states had pulled out of the union and more would follow by the end of 1860. Michigan and Wisconsin threatened secession, but on anti-slavery grounds. The country appeared to be imploding, and the political climate went against President Buchanan.

Wisconsin Governor Alexander Randall declared Buchanan was useless because he refused to take a stand against slave owners. Within the borders of his own state, however, Randall had problems with a militia called the Independent Union Guards that backed President Buchanan. In early March 1860, Randall ordered all guns and munitions of the Union Guard surrendered to the state and per that order, they were seized.

The Union Guard, furious at losing their weapons, scheduled a special excursion trip aboard the *Lady Elgin* to raise money to replace their arms. With many Union Guard members and a large number of their supporters aboard, the calamity led to suspicions of a conspiracy. A persistent allegation making the rounds claimed the sinking of the *Lady Elgin* was no accident.

This much is fact. On September 7, 1860, the day the *Lady Elgin* went down, she was headed north from Chicago with about 300 excursionists, 50 ordinary passengers, and a crew of 35 officers—all bound for Milwaukee. Most of the excursionists were members of the Milwaukee Light Guardsmen, the German Black Jaegers, or the German Green Jaegers, all of whom were returning from a week in Chicago where they tried to raise money for guns and equipment. This group was preparing to join southern forces in the Civil War.

The storm into which the *Lady Elgin* headed when departing Chicago turned into a full-blown, northwesterly gale by 2:00 a.m. The ship was captained by Jack Wilson who was experienced and unconcerned about the storm. He headed directly into the wind and seemed to be handling the turbulence with relative ease.

At 2:30 a.m., the two-masted, lumber schooner *Augusta* burst from the darkness and crashed into the *Lady*'s port side. Darius Malott captained the *Augusta*, and he was traveling downlake on Lake Michigan with a heavy load of lumber he had picked up in Port Huron. His crew may have been busy getting the sails reefed and the ship under control and simply failed to spot the lights of the *Lady Elgin* in time to avoid disaster. Captain Malott ordered the wheelsman to put the wheel over hard to starboard to bring the big schooner around to the wind. The *Augusta* turned, but too slowly to prevent her from slamming hard into the *Lady Elgin* and driving a large hole in the *Lady*'s hull at the midship gangway, just forward of the wheel.

The *Augusta* was badly damaged in the crash. Captain Malott, who should have been celebrating his birthday that day, instead headed his limping vessel to Chicago where he reported the accident. He claimed he had backed off the scene of the collision, and he could not return because his foresails were wrecked, and his bow was badly crushed and leaking. He denied knowing the collision had seriously injured, let alone sank, the *Lady Elgin.*

In the meantime, Captain Wilson tried to salvage his wounded ship. He attempted to get her into shallow water. To gain time, he ordered the cargo and passengers moved to the starboard side. He might be able to repair the hole in the port side if he got the ship to list in the opposite direction. The crew stuffed mattresses into the hole in the hull. The damage, however, was so extensive that these gestures proved useless. Many passengers clung to wreckage from the deck and cabins which floated away from the hull as the ship sank under their feet.

As the *Lady Elgin* hobbled toward the beach, two of the ship's four lifeboats were launched. The first was immediately swamped, and in spite of desperate attempts to keep her afloat, she went under. On the second, it was discovered too late there were no oars. The remaining two lifeboats were never used. Perhaps time ran out. Only 20 minutes passed between the initial strike and the time the *Lady Elgin* vanished in the murky water. Even if the additional lifeboats had been thrown into the thrashing lake, they could have offered only a long shot at survival to no more than 30 or so passengers of the nearly 400 aboard the *Lady.*

Most of the passengers were still alive after the ship sank. They clung to pieces of flotsam. The Lake granted them only a brief reprieve. The gale flung high waves over their bodies bobbing in the icy water. Many of the short-term survivors were exhausted, and after hours of fighting for their lives, they simply gave up. They were among the many drowned. Many more were dashed to their deaths on rocks when they reached the shore. In the brutal game of life and death, the score stood at 98 survivors and more than 300 dead.

A three-month-old infant's body was one of the first to wash ashore after the disaster. Its size and weight undoubtedly made it easy to toss about the waves. The tiny girl's face was said to look content and showed none of the horror etched into the faces of many of the other bodies eventually recovered.

A woman living fifteen miles south of Milwaukee heard the news of the disaster. Believing it had claimed her son, a brother, and a sister, she set out walking seventy-five miles following the railroad track to the morgue set up in Chicago. The Chicago and Milwaukee Railroad offered free passage to anyone traveling to Chicago to identify bodies, but this poor woman was unaware of the offer. With her she carried her nine-month-old son and $5 to buy coffins for her family. She reached her destination, but her money was sufficient to purchase only one coffin. In it she buried her sister. Her brother and son were interred in a pauper's graveyard. Having done what she could, she headed home. She had not gone far when Good Samaritans stopped her and assisted her and the baby to board a train.

An unknown poet pleading for assistance for the families who lost loved ones in the *Lady Elgin* disaster described in a long poetic saga how the mood changed from gaiety to terror that awful night. It reads in part:

How changed every feature, how wild the confusion!
Despair in the darkness and death on the wave!
Some wail for the missing, some plunge, in their madness,
Swift into eternity and their own grave.
"My child!" shrieks a mother; "My daughter," "My father."
And a hundred shrill voices in agony call;
While black grow the waves, with the frantic and struggling,
And faster the boat sinks, beneath her dark pall.

Wreck of the *Lady Elgin*. Courtesy of Pixabay Free Images.

In a postscript to the story of the *Lady Elgin*, the *Augusta* changed her name to the *Colonel Cook* to avoid the stigma of being the ship that sank the *Lady Elgin*. Still, people remembered her part in the awful tragedy. Three years later in 1863, Captain Malott commanded another ship, the *Major*, when it sank in Lake Michigan. The captain did not survive. In a strange quirk of fate, his bones are believed to have come to rest within ten miles of the *Lady Elgin*.

<<>>

The ***Rouse Simmons***, known as the Christmas Tree Ship, sank on November 23, 1912. She continues to stir imaginations more than a century after her wreck and may be the best known of all Lake Michigan disasters. Her story is legend, and she is immortalized in songs, plays, a book, and continuing attempts to trace her last route. There were no survivors of the wreck.

The *Rouse Simmons* is one of the genuine ghost ships of the Great Lakes. A ghost ship is more than a ship that goes down with a loss of lives because such is not an uncommon occurrence. Most of these shipwrecks remain buried and quiet. A true ghost ship is one that is sighted sailing after her demise. *Rouse Simmons* sightings have been reported by sailors for decades. Her sails are tattered as she continues to limp along the Lake Michigan horizon.

The *Rouse Simmons*, a three-masted schooner, was bound for Chicago with a very special cargo that lent her the nickname, The Christmas Tree Ship. She carried 5,500 fresh-cut Christmas trees piled deep in her hold and lashed to the deck. She was a floating forest. The trees were intended for sale from the dock in Chicago where they were expected to spread the Christmas spirit to revelers who purchased them.

The ship was the namesake of Kenosha industrialist Rouse Simmons of Simmons mattress fame. She was built in 1868, was 153-foot long, and weighed 205 tons.

The doomed voyage started with an omen grave enough to cause one crewman to abandon ship. Rats were dropping into the water from the hawser pipe. While landlubbers may think it is a good thing to get rid of rats, when they jump ship, sailors take note. The filthy vermin inhabit ships galleys, and legend warns they desert a sinking ship. If you see them leaving of their own volition, beware. The ship is going down. In this case, it proved true. The *Rouse Simmons* was last spotted on Saturday afternoon with distress signals flying. She sailed south into a blinding snowstorm.

For many years after she sank, the only evidence of the *Rouse Simmons'* fate was pine trees that occasionally became tangled in the nets of commercial fishermen. Then a cork-stopped bottle washed ashore. The message inside read, "Friday. Everybody goodbye. I guess we are all through. Sea washed over our deck board Thursday. During the night, the small boat washed overboard. Leaking bad. Ingvald and Steve fell overboard Thursday. God help us." –Herman Schuenemann. The note appeared to be part of the captain's log.

In 1924 twelve years after the Simmons went down, Captain Schuenemann's wallet caught in a fishing net. The contents were intact and legible due to the oilskin that encased it and the rubber band that held it tight. It rekindled memories of the sweet-natured and beloved man who dealt in Yuletide cheer. But the captain may have had a fatal character flaw that contributed to his undoing. Whether it was greed, hardheadedness, or a desire to spread happiness, it was reported that he overloaded the boat with trees to the point where one crewman warned that if they encountered a storm, the boat would be too top heavy to pull through. The captain ignored the warning.

In 1927 a second bottle washed ashore. Inside was a note that read, "These lines are written at 10:30 p.m. Schooner H.S. ready to go down about 20 miles southeast of Two Rivers Point between fifteen or twenty miles off shore. All hands lashed to one line. Goodbye."—Charles Nelson. (The H.S. refers to Herman Schuenemann.)

While the *Rouse Simmons* had no radio, and the wreck left no survivors, it was as though the ghosts of this tragedy reached from their watery grave and communicated their story to the living through two notes in bottles and an intact wallet.

The site of the wreck remained a mystery until 1971 when salvager Ken Bellrichard of Milwaukee discovered the *Rouse Simmons* in 180 feet of water off Rawley Point. Her bones remain nearly intact, and she lies at rest, upright on the floor of the lake. Her cargo hold is still filled with the shrunken remains of Christmas trees.

Captain Schuenemann's wife and daughters continued selling Christmas trees from the deck of a schooner in the Chicago harbor for many years after his death. But the time of Christmas Tree Ships was almost at an end. Wholesale tree farms and better transportation on railroads and highways ended the holiday tradition where revelers headed to the harbor to choose their tree from the deck of a ship.

Captain Schuenemann's widow lived more than 20 years after his death and upon her death, was laid to rest next to her husband in a Chicago cemetery. Their joint headstone bears a tiny engraved Christmas tree between their names.

<<>>

The ***Eastland*** remains the oddest tragedy ever to befall a ship on Lake Michigan. She met her demise on July 24, 1915, but not due to a raging storm or even in open water.

The *Eastland* was tied to the dock at the Clark Street Bridge in the narrow channel of the Chicago River when tragedy befell her. She was a relatively young ship, with only ten years of service on the lakes. She weighed 1,900 tons. Captain Harry Pederson was at her helm.

The channel was as unlikely a spot for this senseless mishap as could have been envisioned. The *Eastland* was preparing to transport 2,500 Western Electric Company passengers to a pleasant holiday across the beautiful lake to the Michigan dunes. Some estimates conclude that perhaps there were 3,000 aboard the ship designed to carry only 2,500. The final investigation determined that overcrowding was not a significant issue in the disaster.

Passengers began boarding at 7:00 a.m. to get an early start on the day's festivities. Ragtime music floated in the air as happy revelers stowed picnic baskets and engaged in lighthearted chatter with friends and colleagues. Skies were overcast with spitting drizzle, but the precipitation could not dampen the spirits of travelers on holiday. Only those on the main deck heard the cries, "Look out, the boat's turning over!" For the moment, it barely caused a pause in their conversations, so certain were those aboard that the cry must be in jest.

But something was definitely amiss. The great ship tilted toward the dock. Captain Pederson attempted to correct the situation and ordered the sea cocks opened to tip the ship. She uprighted but then listed at a dangerous angle away from the dock. Passengers who had gone below found themselves smashing against the bulkheads. Bottles and other loose items crashed about. Chairs on deck slid from starboard to port. The icebox in the refreshment stand tore loose and skidded across the deck.

Many passengers fearing for their lives jumped overboard. By 7:30 a.m., the demon-possessed ship overturned in the river with her starboard side upward above the water. Passengers caught in the confusion panicked. Many drowned within a few feet of the dock. Hundreds more were trapped in cabins below the decks. A few lucky passengers crawled through portholes, and a few more were still alive when rescuers with acetylene torches cut a path to safety.

No satisfactory reason has been offered to explain the erratic behavior of an otherwise predictable ship. One of the first theories was that the passengers all crowded to one side to watch a tug pass. That theory was discarded at the inquest. Improper ballast may have been the cause, but no one will ever know for sure. The ship was in fine condition and continued to sail after the tragic incident. She was renamed the *U.S.S. Wilmette* and was converted to a naval training ship. Most who saw her moored at the Randolph Street dock in Chicago had no indication that the *U.S.S. Wilmette* had been the *Eastland* in her prior life. They simply stood and admired her clean lines and sharp appearance.

Captain Pederson and steamship company officials were charged with criminal negligence, but a U. S. Circuit Court of Appeals ultimately issued a decision that the boat was seaworthy, and the operators had acted appropriately. That decision closed the legal aspect of the case. It did not close the public's indignation that the ship had caused the loss of half as many lives as had been doomed on the *Titanic* three years earlier with no satisfactory explanation. The *Titanic* could be explained, an iceberg, a cocky attitude that she was unsinkable, a speed to set records, and a lack of visibility. But, the *Eastland*? She had never moved out of the channel. It was unthinkable.

The ship, however, had been the target of ugly rumors about her safety for years. So persistent were the stories, that the owners of the *Eastland* resorted to taking out a half-page advertisement in the *Cleveland Plain Dealer* on August 9, 1910. The ad praised the ship for her strength, her safety record, and the joy her excursions had brought to thousands of happy, satisfied passengers. It went on to offer a $5,000 reward, "we offer the above reward to any person that will bring forth a naval engineer, a marine architect, a ship builder, or anyone qualified to pass judgment on the merits of a ship who will say that the steamer *Eastland* is not a seaworthy ship, or that she would not ride out any storm, or weather any condition that can arise on either lake or ocean."

Whatever the cause, on a hot steamy day in July, the *Eastland* became possessed, and more than 800 people died, among them 22 entire families. Those gruesome statistics earned her the dubious distinction of the worst loss of lives in one accident on the Great Lakes. It was a record that would hopefully never be broken.

24. Menominee

Menominee had a 2020 population of 8,599. It is the first Michigan city along the northwestern coast of Lake Michigan. Menominee and Marinette, Wisconsin, are often called twin cities, and they share a hospital, newspaper, and chamber of commerce. The cities, one on either side of the interstate bridge over the Menominee River, work together to benefit their two cities, two counties, and two states. The current bridge, built in 1929, replaced earlier bridges that connected the communities.

Menominee took its name from the Menominee Native Americans who at one time lived in the area. The Menominee called themselves the *Mamaceqtaw* which translates as "the people." They called their village *Menikaneh* which means "at the good village."

The Menominee were neighbors to the Ojibwe, a tribe that had migrated from the Atlantic coast when their Great Spirit told them to travel west in canoes until they came to the place where rice grew on water. The Menominee harvested rice as a dietary staple. A second theory for the derivation of the name Menominee is that it is an English translation of the Ojibwe words "wild rice," and so Menominee was the name by which the Ojibwe called their neighbors.

The Menominee were removed west of the Mississippi River to a reservation along the Wolf River in Wisconsin after they ceded their territory in Michigan to the United States by the Treaty of Cedars in 1836.

Dudley Bug.
Courtesy of wikimedia.org.

During the 1800s, Menominee became a prosperous lumber community that at one time produced more lumber than any other city in the United States. From 1913 to 1915, the Dudley Manufacturing Company operated in Menominee where it produced the Dudley Bug, a gas-powered, wood, two-seater car. Only 100 of the vehicles were manufactured.

Menominee needed to diversify its manufacturing base and garnered the attention of inventor Marshal Burns Lloyd of Minneapolis whose company made wicker baby buggies. Lloyd wanted to construct buggies that were softer, more durable, and more comfortable. In 1917 he invented an automated loom that is still in use today. He began making other furniture, pieces of which grace the White House, Camp David, the vice president's residence, and the homes of many wealthy and famous people including Kathy Lee Gifford, Martha Stewart, and Dolly Parton.

In 1940 Menominee citizens joined a spoof nominating Gracie Allen, the female half of Burns and Allen, as mayor of their city. The comedy duo had announced her candidacy for president of the United States on the Surprise Party ticket. Gracie was disqualified as a mayoral candidate because she was not a resident of Menominee. One of Gracie's memorable one-liners from her presidential campaign came when she was asked about Lend-Lease, and she famously said, "I don't know much about the Lend-Lease Bill, but if we owe it, we should pay it."

• MUSEUMS

Bailey Park and the West Shore Fishing Museum, N5156 State Highway M-35, 15 miles north of Menominee, was once the site of the Charles L. Bailey commercial fishery. The fishery was located next door to the Bailey family's homestead which included a house, chicken coop, and carriage shed. The buildings were in poor condition, but in 1997 the Bailey Property Preservation Association, a group of dedicated volunteers, took on the task of restoring the structures. The result is a museum worthy of a tourist's time. Filled with fishing artifacts including five commercial fishing boats, the museum workers greet you and share a fascinating glimpse into the fishing industry of the past. Pretty gardens grace the grounds, and at times plants are sold to visitors. There is a gift shop on premises.

<<>>

The **Menominee County Historical Society Heritage Museum**, 904 11th Avenue. In 1976 the Menominee County Historical Society acquired the St. John the Baptist Catholic Church for use as a heritage museum. The hardworking volunteers turned the interior into a repository for priceless artifacts and photographs from Menominee County's history.

County Historical Society Heritage Museum inside the former St. John the Baptist Catholic Church.
Courtesy of Bob Royce.

• Beaches, Parks, and Trails

John Henes Park, Henes Park Drive, provides a one-way, paved driving loop with places to stop and savor the view or go for a hike. Situated on the lake, the park has picnic shelters, grills, a playground, a sand volleyball court, and a beach area.

<<>>

Tourist Beach, 90 Harbor Drive, is a quiet, mostly undeveloped beach, and a good place to find beach glass. It is located downtown near the lighthouse. (See North Pier Light.) It is also close to a quaint shopping area. Tourist Beach may be the sandiest beach in Menominee, but the only facilities are restrooms.

• Other Stops to Consider

Holy Spirit Catholic Church, 1016 10th Avenue, is an interesting drive-by. If you are in the neighborhood look for the red brick church with the tall steeple.

<<>>

Walking Tour of Menominee's Historic District. You can find a walking tour map online or simply head downtown to First Street. The historic district includes First Street from Fourth to Tenth Avenue. You will be treated to an eclectic mix of architecture.

Menominee Courthouse. Courtesy of Bob Royce.

• LIGHTHOUSE

North Pier Light.
Courtesy of Bob Royce.

The **Menominee North Pier Light**, Harbor Drive, built in 1877, was the first to guide ships into the Menominee River. The current tower was built in 1927 and still assists vessels entering the river's ship canal. The 34-foot tower is a local icon. In 2008 the U.S. Coast Guard turned over possession of the light station to the City of Menominee.

With private donors and willing volunteers, several projects have improved the light station's physical condition and opened it to the public. The historical society provides tours of the interior.

• SHIPWRECK

The ***Plymouth***, a schooner lumber barge with a seven-man crew, went down during the big storm of November 13, 1913. She was in the tow of the tug *James A. Martin* when the storm struck. Questions remain. Did Captain Louis Stetunsky of the *Martin* desert the *Plymouth*? Did he seek shelter believing the *Plymouth* was stable? Did he intend to return when the storm abated?

The two vessels cleared the Menominee Light before they were forced to seek shelter. In an effort to keep the barge from crashing on the rocks, the tug towed it to nearby Gull Island where it was anchored. What happened after that depends upon the story you accept. It is undisputed that the *Martin* left the *Plymouth* and headed for the shelter of Summer Island passage where the *Martin* anchored to wait out the storm.

A few days later, Captain Stetunsky caused a sensation when he arrived in Menominee with his tug battered and bruised, looking much worse for the storm but miraculously afloat. Bystanders thought they saw ghosts. Everyone assumed the *Martin* and the *Plymouth* had gone down together in the maniacal gale.

Captain Stetunsky described the horror that he and his crew of eight suffered in the preceding days. The storm had started on Thursday and Stetunsky made no headway hauling the barge against the worsening weather. He attempted to anchor both ships in the lee of St. Martins Island. Unable to achieve the degree of security he wanted, he hauled the barge to a spot off Gull Island that he felt offered better anchorage.

Here the two versions of this account diverge. Stetunsky insisted that only when the barge appeared to be riding safely, did he seek better refuge for his tug in the Summer

Island passage. He was not leaving the *Plymouth* to whatever fate might befall her. The *Martin* lacked power to battle the storm and tow the barge. It was evident to him that both ships would founder if they remained tethered to one another. As it was, he had barely survived. He never mentioned why he did not take the crew of the *Plymouth* aboard his tug, but perhaps he did not consider one ship safer than the other.

Three days after the storm quelled, Captain Stetunsky returned to the spot he had left the *Plymouth* anchored. The barge had vanished. He sailed on to Menominee.

After several days, parts of the lost ship began washing ashore—a hatch cover here, a piece of the cabin there. Broken lifeboats from the *Plymouth* were found in Ludington.

Skeptics argued that Captain Stetunsky abandoned the *Plymouth* and left her crew to perish. The evidence supporting this allegation arrived two weeks after the *Plymouth* vanished. A bottle was found five miles from Pentwater. Inside was a message, "Dear wife and Children. We were left up here in Lake Michigan by McKinnon, Captain *James H. Martin*, tug, at anchor. He went away and never said goodbye or anything to us. Lost one man yesterday. We have been out in storm forty hours. Goodbye dear ones, I might see you in Heaven. Pray for me. Chris K." Chris Keenan's body was found several days later on a beach near Manistee.

While the note has some facts wrong (Captain McKinnon instead of Stetunsky) the authenticity of the message has never been questioned, and under any interpretation it seems clear the author of that note felt abandoned, whether he was or was not.

• The Famous or Infamous with Ties to Menominee

No one from Menominee seems slated to be a major player in the annals of history. There are a handful of notables who are respected in their hometown.

Sports figures

Dave Mason, NFL player (Minnesota Vikings, New England Patriots, and Green Bay Packers); John McLean, Olympic silver medal winner; **Fred Stephenson Norcross**, University of Michigan football captain, coach at Oregon State University; **Bill Rademacher**, NFL player, Super Bowl III champion; **Leonard J. Umnus**, college football player and coach.

<<>>

Politicians

Audrey Cleary, North Dakota State Legislator; **Kent T. Lundgren**, pharmacist and Michigan state senator; **Richard P. Matty**, Wisconsin State Assemblyman; **Samuel M. Stephenson**, member of United States House of Representatives from Michigan; **Bart Stupak**, member of U.S. House of Representatives from Michigan.

<<>>

The Arts

Kathleen Kirkham, silent film actress; **Mitchell Leisen**, Hollywood director, art director and costumer designer; **Doris Packer**, actress (played Mrs. Rayburn, Theodore Cleaver's principal in the television series *Leave It to Beaver)*; **Mitzi Shore**, Los Aneles Comedy Store.

<<>>

Educators

Alvin H. Nielsen, molecular spectroscopist; **Harald Herborg Nielsen**, physicist; **Robyn Leigh Tanguay**, molecular toxicologist, Oregon State University.

<<>>

And finally, **William Nolde**, the last American soldier killed in Vietnam before the ceasefire. (Other soldiers were killed after the ceasefire.) Nolde, born in Menominee, is buried in Arlington.

• Books with Ties to Menominee

Several books have been written about the plight, history, and survival of the Menominee Native Americans.

Raymond Kaquatosh, ***Little Hawk and the Lone Wolf: A Memoir***, is a coming-of-age story of a Menominee boy raised on the reservation in Wisconsin nearly a century after his forefathers were relocated there when the tribe ceded its land to the United States.

<<>>

Emily Hemstock, ***Identified: A Menominee Michigan Novel***, is the story of Chloe Wyatt, a Menominee high school student facing the question of what she wants to be when she grows up. Her lawyer-dad throws out the possibility of being a spy. Chloe is kidnapped which puts the question in a different perspective.

• Ghost Stories (an unusual creature)

The **Menominee Sasquatch** is reported to be a large hairy or fur-covered, ape-like creature seen by many in the Menominee area. The numerous sightings give credence to, or at least support for, the age-old legends of local Native Americans who have long described such a beast.

Although many countries have some version of a Sasquatch (Abominable Snowman, Yeti), the United States version featured a humanoid-like animal that roamed from British Columbia to Northern California, and to a lesser extent throughout North America. There has been an explosion of reported sightings, including in most Michigan counties.

Referred to as a cryptid, a creature whose existence is suggested but not yet confirmed, the Upper Peninsula

Bigfoot/Sasquatch Research Organization, located in Menominee, is dedicated to finding proof that Bigfoot is real and living in the U.P.

A Menominee couple, the Sulks, report several sightings and have taken what they claim to be pictures of the Sasquatch. Their story has captured the attention of *Animal Planet* for their episode, Finding Bigfoot. The story starts in March 2019 when the Sulks set up a series of cameras on their wooded property to capture photos of local wildlife. They claim they were unprepared for what they saw when they examined their shadowy photo. They declare the picture is that of Sasquatch.

Complicating any serious attempts to credit or discredit the Sasquatch stories, are the folks who don furs and prowl the forest, in spite of the risk of being shot by a startled hunter. There may never be answers to whether Sasquatch exists, but two things are certain, 1) there have been lots of stories and reportings, so you could conclude that where there's smoke there's fire, and 2) Sasquatch doesn't seem to be a violent sort of forest predator. Still, if you walk through the forest and encounter him, it's probably best to backtrack, and if you prefer not to risk being called crazy, keep the story to yourself.

25. Escanaba

Escanaba, sometimes called Esky, boasted a 2020 population of 12,141 making it the third largest city in the Upper Peninsula. It is located on the Escanaba River and Little Bay de Noc. Big and Little Bays de Noc are at the upper end of Lake Michigan's Green Bay. They make up about 100,000 acres of prime sportfishing water. The bays are best known for large and plentiful walleye, but many other fish are caught there. The Bays de Noc call themselves the walleye capital of the world. Boaters are drawn to the safe harbor, and their fishing efforts are seldom disappointed.

Escanaba is named for the Escanaba River which got its name from Ojibwe words that translated mean something like "Land of the Red Buck."

Surveyor Eli Royce was the first European to settle in the port town of Escanaba. He arrived in 1863. As with many Upper Peninsula towns, lumber was the original mainstay of the economy, followed by iron that came from the Marquette Range and was shipped on Escanaba barges. In 1936 Escanaba harvested and processed 100,000 square feet of birdseye maple for the English luxury liner, the *Queen Mary*.

As shipping increased, a lighthouse was needed to warn of sand shoals in Little Bay de Noc. The U.S. Lighthouse Service responded by approving the Sand Point Lighthouse.

Tourism has become big business as people discover the white sand beaches. Local wineries may not produce wines to rival California's Napa Valley, but they do offer an enjoyable experience.

The city of Escanaba provides many cultural outlets for its citizens and invites visitors to enjoy the William Bonifas Fine Arts Center and the Waterfront Art Festival, and performances of the Players de Noc, the Bay de Noc Choral Society, and the Escanaba City Band.

• Museum

The Delta County Historical Museum, 16 Water Plant Road (behind the lighthouse), opened in 1956. The museum began collecting and displaying artifacts of Delta County inhabitants and their history of logging, shipping, railway industry, military, and Native American culture in a step-by-step progression from founding to current. Seasonal hours.

• Beaches, Parks, and Trails

Ludington Park, 1007 Ludington Street, provides waterfront views, multiple beach areas, paved trails, fishing areas, picnic spots, a 22,500 square foot playground constructed of wood, and a gazebo, fountain, and band shell for summer concerts. The large park has three quarters of a mile of lakeshore where the city's easternmost point extends into Little Bay de Noc.

<<>>

Escanaba Municipal Beach, located on Aronson Island, is open seasonally. Amenities include a small playground, picnic area, beach house with changing area, restrooms, and showers. Kayak and paddleboard rental. Day passes available for boat launch.

• Other Stops to Consider

Churches of Escanaba. This might be the city to take a church tour. Escanaba has several historic churches with interesting architecture.

▪ **Bethany Lutheran Church**, 202 South 11th Street, a two-towered, brick church with a stained-glass window. Originally founded in 1879 as the Swedish Evangelical Lutheran Church, the current church building was constructed in 1912. The land on which the church stands was given by Nels Ludington of Chicago's Ludington Lumber Company.

▪ **First Presbyterian Church**, 819 1st Avenue South, a stately colossal of dark red brick with a Celtic cross on the exterior.

▪ **St. Joseph and St. Patrick Catholic Church**, 709 1st Avenue, a beige brick edifice with interesting exterior doors.

▪ **First United Methodist Church**, 302 South 6th Street, a smaller church that has stood on the same corner for more than a century.

<<>>

House of Ludington Hotel and Historical Marker. Courtesy of Bob Royce.

The **House of Ludington**, 223 Ludington Street, is a well-known landmark in Escanaba. Take a peek as you continue your architectural drive through the city. Built in 1865 and called the Gaynor House Hotel which bragged it was the only hotel in the area offering baths, the hotel was renamed in 1871 to honor the locally prominent lumberman Nelson Ludington. In 1883 the hotel was rebuilt as a brick structure in the Queen Anne Style and was renamed the New Ludington Hotel. Local stories claim that during prohibition, Al Capone utilized the tunnels underneath the basement of the hotel. The hotel is currently a Michigan Historic Site.

• LIGHTHOUSE

Sand Point Lighthouse, 16 Water Plant Road on the same property as the Delta County Historical Museum, was built in 1867 by the National Lighthouse Service. The light warned ships of the dangerous sand reef in the bay. The Sand Point Lighthouse served mariners from 1868 until 1939 except for a few months in 1886 when a suspicious fire damaged the building. The blaze took the life of keeper

Mary Terry. (See Famous or Infamous with Ties to Escanaba.)

The Sand Point Lighthouse was deactivated in 1939. Nine keepers and their families had lived in the lighthouse and kept the light shining out over Little Bay De Noc during the light's 71 years of active service. Following deactivation, the building was used by the Coast Guard as a residence for its servicemen. In 1985 the Coast Guard discontinued use of the building. Razing the structure was considered. The Delta County Historical Society stepped in to save one of the oldest and most historic buildings in the area.

A lease from the Coast Guard was negotiated, and research for restoration and fundraising began. The building was completely restored to its original design of the late 1860s and is now open to the public along with the museum. It is listed on the National Register of Historic Places.

Sand Point Lighthouse. Courtesy of Bob Royce.

• The Famous or Infamous with Ties to Escanaba

Tom Bissell, author and Guggenheim Fellow, was born in Escanaba in 1974. He was a frequent reviewer for *The New York Times* Book Review and wrote for *Harper's Magazine* and *The New Republic.* While much of his writing was considered travel writing and autobiographical, Bissell also authored several books including *Chasing the Sea; Lost Among the Ghosts of Empire in Central Asia*; *Speak, Commentary; The Big Little Book of Fake DVD Commentaries*; *God Lives in St. Petersburg: and Other Stories; The Father of All Things: A Marine, His Son, and the Legacy of Vietnam*; *Extra Lives: Why Video Games Matter*; *Magic Hours: Essays On Creators and Creation*; *The Disaster Artist: My Life Inside The Room; The Greatest Bad Movie Ever Made*; *Apostle: Travels Among the Tombs of the Twelve*; and *Everything About Everything: Infinite Jest, and Twenty Years Later.*

<<>>

Mary Terry was the first lighthouse keeper of the Sand Point Lighthouse. She performed her duties for 18 years and was one of the first women lighthouse keepers on the Great Lakes.

Mary's husband, John, was appointed to the position of keeper while the lighthouse was under construction. He died of consumption before the light's completion, and Mary was officially appointed to take his place. Childless and a widow, she lived alone in the lighthouse and kept the beacon shining during even the worst of winter storms.

In March 1886, fire severely damaged the building and killed Mary. The blaze raised eyebrows in the community where many people thought Mary had been murdered, robbed, and the lighthouse set on fire to cover the crime.

Speculation was supported by the south lighthouse door found open, the bolt of the door's lock pushed forward as though the door had been forced open, and Mary's body discovered in the oil room rather than her bedroom which is where she would have been expected to be at that time of night. Mary was a cautious and meticulous woman; one people couldn't imagine carelessly causing a fire.

An article in the local paper quoted the coroner, "Mrs. Terry came to her death from causes and by means unknown."

<<>>

The **Bigamist Pirate of the Great Lakes, Roarin' Dan Seavey**. Escanaba has its share of politicians, sports figures, and civic leaders. But the most notorious character with ties to the city is a pirate. Dan Seavey's life wasn't a clear course down the straight and narrow from birth in 1865 to death in a nursing home 84 years later. Instead, his years took twisting, turning, meandering paths where he dabbled in both the legal and illegal, and many times it was hard to figure out which he favored.

Dan may not have been the equal of swashbuckling Jack Sparrow, but he was no slouch in the looks department. He was tall with a muscular upper torso, long arms, big hands and a slim lower body. His freckled complexion dealt him a boyish appeal. More than one woman at a harbor port of call described him as the most handsome man around.

For the first thirty years of Dan's life, no one foresaw what was to come. He ran away from home at 13 and joined the U.S. Navy as soon as they'd take him, but those facts painted the picture of a man who liked adventure and could take care of himself, not signs of an evolving criminal.

In his early 20s, Dan married a 14-year-old girl, but it was a different time, and that wasn't unheard of either. The couple settled in Milwaukee, Wisconsin, and started a family.

Dan tried his hand at farming, fishing, and running a saloon, all respectable, or semi-respectable pursuits, to support his wife and two young daughters. Then, in 1898

Dan got gold fever. His adventurous spirit revved up, and he took off to the Klondike Gold Rush. He left Milwaukee without a backward glance or a word of goodbye to his wife or kids. Perhaps he planned to return home a hero.

Within two years, he moved back to the lower states, this time to Michigan, specifically Escanaba. With the little stash of money that stood between him and complete destitution, he bought a boat he called the *Wanderer*, found himself a new wife without bothering to divorce the first Mrs. Seavey, and took up a new business—pirate of the Great Lakes. He didn't announce his career plans or give his new occupation that name, just subtly wove criminal activities with his law-abiding pursuits. His cargo hold transported legitimate goods along with stolen lumber and illegally hunted venison, the latter, in some places, considered a highly-desired delicacy.

A competitor who saw the profit in hawking poached venison died knowing that Dan was as lethal as he was good-looking. Dan shot his cannon at the hapless rival's ship, killing all aboard.

Sometimes to set up his mark—a ship Seavey intended to rob—he pulled a nasty trick called moon cussing. He anchored the *Wanderer* alongside a shoal or reef and attached lights to his boat, giving unsuspecting ships the mistaken impression that they were near port. After luring a ship into his trap, Dan boarded the crippled vessel and helped himself to whatever treasures it carried.

Perhaps Dan's most amazing escapade happened in the port of Grand Haven. The story is so mired in mismatched snippets of information that it's difficult to sort truth from fiction. But some elements of the tale are beyond dispute.

Roarin' Dan was in harbor drinking on June 11, 1908. So was much of the crew and Captain McCormick of the schooner *Nellie Johnson*. It is unclear if Dan was part of the *Johnson*'s crew, but he drank with them, buying round after round of alcohol while he remained calculatingly sober. As the night progressed, he convinced two of the *Johnson* crew members to mutiny, help him seize the ship, run it to Chicago, and sell its cargo of cedar posts. Crew members who did not join the scheme were thrown overboard into the harbor. The theft was accomplished without a hitch.

But his luck had temporarily run out. He arrived in the Windy City and was unable to sell the timber. Aboard a stolen vessel loaded with useless merchandise, he headed back uplake. Before long, he noticed lawmen following in his wake.

Captain McCormick, when he awoke from his drunken stupor, had been horrified to find his boat gone. He notified authorities, and the first warrant ever issued for piracy on the Great Lakes was sworn out against Seavey. If caught and convicted, Roarin' Dan faced a federal capital crime and could be hung, even though Michigan by that time had no death penalty.

Captain Preston Uberroth entered the fray. He was assigned the unusual case of a stolen ship with a mutinous crew aboard. Uberroth, a man with a long career with the Revenue Cutter Services,[6] had taken command of the Great Lakes Cutter *Tuscarora* in 1907. Six months later, from that vessel, he gave chase to pirate Seavey.

Uberroth was aided in his mission of retrieving the *Nellie Johnson* by Deputy Marshall Thomas Currier, an experienced manhunter. The trio, McCormick, Uberroth, and Currier, was soon in hot pursuit, although for a good portion of the race, they lagged one port behind the *Johnson*.

Two weeks after the hijacking, the *Tuscarora*'s lawmen spotted the *Johnson* in the port of Frankfort. They boarded, and found she had six feet of water in her hold, but her

[6] The Revenue Cutter Services later combined with the Lifesaving Service to become the U.S. Coast Guard.

cargo remained intact. Pirate Seavey had deserted the ship and returned to his vessel, the *Wanderer.* The pirate hoisted both sails trying to catch every gust of light wind. The *Tuscarora* gave such spirited a chase that the paint burned off her smokestack. Details of the quest's final hour are not entirely clear. Cannons were reportedly fired. If true, no one was injured, and the ships sustained no damage. Pirate Dan who had now established his chosen career path, surrendered, was placed in irons, and returned to Chicago where he was charged with mutiny and revolt.

Seavey's defense was that he did not steal the *Nellie Johnson.* He won her in a poker game. Two weeks later Dan was acquitted and back in Frankfort wearing a huge grin and a new suit of clothes. The stories of how the most notorious pirate on the lakes went free vary from account to account. Maybe he secured legal counsel from a cunning Chicago lawyer to plead his case. Maybe the authorities bought his cockamamie poker story. And maybe Captain McCormick never showed up to testify.

Roarin' Dan Seavey at age 55 in 1920.
Photo in the Public Domain.

But there was still more to the story. The government decided something had to be done about the illegal activity on the lakes. They had just the man to help them tame the waters. Dan Seavey. Just like that, Pirate Dan became Marshall Dan.

During the next decades of his life, Dan may have worn two hats, one a law-biding government man, and the other a thief who never gave up trying to make a buck on ill-gotten goods. If the gold rush had proven disappointing, prohibition was a pirate's bonanza. Dan traded hooch for money and guns in Chicago and Detroit. Other stories say he suffered disabling burns during a sawmill fire and retired. Some insisted he had a come-to-Jesus awakening and crossed completely to the side of truth and justice.

Seavey married a third time, although what happened to any of his three wives is murky. In the late 1920s, he went to live with his daughter in Peshtigo, Wisconsin. He remained with her until he entered Eklund Nursing Home where he died in 1949. If his first family held a grudge because he deserted them, it doesn't seem to fit with the known facts. His daughter is buried alongside him in the Forest Home Cemetery in Marinette, Wisconsin.

And that's the tale of Roaring Dan-the-murdering-thieving-bigamist-marshal-pirate of the Great Lakes.

• A Play and A Movie set in Escanaba

Escanaba in da Moonlight, written and directed by Jeff Daniels, is the story of a family's angst on the eve of deer hunting season. The comedy centers around the misfortune of the oldest son who has never succeeded in bagging his buck.

26. Gladstone

Gladstone, 2020 population of 4,702, heralds itself as a Year-Round Playground. Located beside Little Bay de Noc on the northern Lake Michigan shore, the city has reason for such a boast. Originally called *Minnewasca* by the Soo Line Railroad that serviced the area, the name meant "white water" in the Ojibwe language. When the name was filed with the county and Secretary of State, it was changed to Gladstone to honor the British premier, William Evert Gladstone.

Until the mid-nineteenth century, the area around Gladstone was inhabited by Ojibwe, with only an occasional European or American fur trader or fisherman. The town was settled in 1859 when the Hamilton Corporation of Fayette used it as a shipping port for transporting iron ore. Transport of lumber, coal, and copper helped turn Gladstone into a busy place.

Gladstone was incorporated and became a village in 1887, and two years later became a city.

• Beaches, Parks, and Trails

Days River Natural Trail, three miles northwest of Gladstone at US 2 and Days River Road. Day's River Nature Trail is a 9.3-mile trail. It is enjoyed for hiking, biking, running, snowshoeing, and cross-country skiing. Five loops offer increasing levels of difficulty. The first two are easy and child-friendly. Several single tracks off the main path add challenge for mountain bikers. The main trail winds through pine, spruce, and cedar ridges with trees marked with identification signs. Along the way, it is likely you'll spot Michigan's famous white-tailed deer, hawks, eagle, and other wildlife.

<<>>

Gladstone Harbor at Van Cleve Park, 1224 Lake Shore Drive, provides boat launch and amenities for both transient and seasonal boaters. Amenities include wireless internet, holding tank pump-out service, ice, restrooms, showers, picnic tables, and grills.

• The Famous or Infamous with Ties to Gladstone

Becky Iverson, professional golfer, was born in Escanaba and lived in Gladstone. She played on the LPGA tour.

<<>>

Frank Smith, cartoon animator and film director, was born in Gladstone on August 31, 1911. He worked on Popeye and Betty Boop cartoons and in 1951 won an Oscar for *Gerald McBoing-Boing.* In association with director/ producer Bill Melendez, he animated several *Peanuts* television specials.

27. Fayette Historic State Park

A Michigan Ghost Town, Fayette may have become a ghost town, but it is a ghost town with attitude and character, sitting on the shore of Lake Michigan's Snail Shell Harbor. With the sun shining, the water is a most ethereal color of blue. Wildflowers add a splash of color, and the majestic trees act as sentries protecting everything in sight. White-tailed deer nibble clover, and it isn't unusual to see a large herd along the tree line at sunset.

Fayette Historic State Park, between Snail Shell Harbor and Sand Bay on the southern side of the Upper Peninsula on Lake Michigan, is a state park listed on the National Register of Historic Places.

In the mid and late-1800s, Jackson Iron Company was a productive iron-smelting operation with two blast furnaces and several charcoal kilns. Located nearby was the limestone needed to purify the iron ore. A large dock facilitated shipment of the iron. The company expected a rosy future. In its 24 years of operation, the blast furnaces of the small village produced 229,288 tons of iron.

Fayette grew up around its singular industry, and following the Civil War, it drew nearly 500 residents to live and work there. But the venture that had started on such an optimist note in 1867, closed its doors in 1891, the result of the declining market and depletion of the hardwoods needed for fuel.

Residents were forced to look for other employment. Some managed to eke out a living farming and fishing. In 1916 an investor turned the village into a summer resort, and it continued in that capacity until 1946 when ownership changed hands, and the new manager fell behind in taxes. The next chapter of the story included the sale to Escanaba Paper Company that swapped it to the Michigan government for timberland. The state turned it into a park in 1959.

Today, the village has been reconstructed as a living museum that showcases life in this part of the Upper Peninsula in the late 1800s. More than 20 buildings are open to visitors.

The park offers campsites with electrical service and access to vault toilets and water. Boat camping is allowed in Snail Shell Harbor. Sand Bay, a short distance from campsites, has a beach on Lake Michigan. A picnic area with tables and grills is adjacent to the beach. A playground is available for children, and the park features approximately five miles of hiking trails.

The village is open seasonally and requires a Michigan State Park Permit. Your first stop should be the visitors center and your last the museum store.

28. Kitch-iti-kipi

Located at the northern terminus of state highway M-149, a 15-minute drive north of US 2 at Thompson. Off the beaten path as you follow Michigan's Waterways, this stop is worth the 12-mile detour inland. Discover Kitch-iti-kipi just as John Bellaire did over a century ago. Kitch-iti-kipi is translated several ways including the Great Water, the Blue Sky I See, the Roaring Bubbling Spring, Heaven's Mirror, or as commonly interpreted, the Big Spring.

Bellaire came from Seney when his lumbering days ended. The white pine had been overharvested, and he needed a new line of work. He opened a dime store in nearby Manistique. As his luck, and ours, would have it, he found more than a new career. He stumbled across a tangle of trees and vegetation covering piles of rubbish left by previous lumbermen. He looked closely at what the detritus obscured.

Kitch-iti-kipi. Courtesy of Bob Royce.

The treasure was Michigan's largest freshwater spring, more than 200 feet across and 40 feet deep. Bellaire couldn't have told you at the time, but his discovery gushed more than 10,000 gallons a minute from fissures in the underlying limestone.

Why was this our good fortune? Well, Bellaire could have purchased the property and kept it for himself, but Bellaire was a man with an altruistic disposition. He recognized that a natural gem was hidden in the debris and decaying vegetation. He felt everyone should see this special place. He so enjoyed sharing his discovery that he often closed his store to take a new visitor to the site.

In 1926 he struck a course of action grander than taking one visitor at a time. Through Frank Book, who represented the Palms Book Land Company, Bellaire arranged to sell almost 90 acres of the land around and including the big spring to the State of Michigan for $10.

There was a condition. The deed stipulated that the property must be forever used as a public park. It was called Palms Book State Park. Additional land has been annexed to the park since that time, some by land transfer, some as a result of delinquent taxes. The park is now 388 acres.

At Kitch-iti-kipi, the spring water never freezes and stays at a constant 45 degrees. The park is open year-round and is a favorite of snowmobilers, cross-country skiers, and snowshoers. The sight of that emerald-colored water set against the snow-covered trees and terrain provides a picture unlike any other. The water is so clear that you can see the gushing-water creating sandy swirls on the bottom.

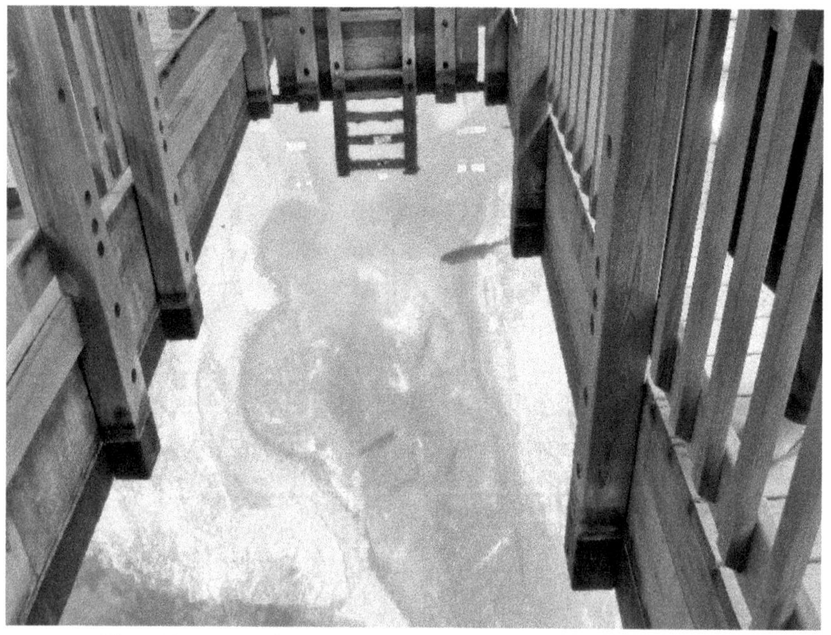

Glass Bottom Observation Raft. Courtesy of Bob Royce.

A self-operated observation raft transports you from a small dock into the spring. It is powered by pulleys operated either by a park employee or a visitor. The glass bottom of the raft lets you see trout swimming among ancient mineral-encrusted trees and branches resting on the bottom.

This is a day park, although there is camping at Indian Lake State Park about seven miles away. Amenities at Kitch-iti-kipi include a shaded picnic area, modern toilet facilities, and the Palms Book Trading Post where you can buy souvenirs, ice cream, and beverages. You will need a state park permit for admission.

Kitch-iti-kipi Dock and Observation Platform.
Courtesy of Bob Royce.

Kitch-iti-kipi comes with a legend. The most prevalent story tells about a Native American chieftain who had fallen in love with a beautiful young woman from his tribe. She trifled with his feelings, and knowing her charms affected men to do crazy things, she told him he had to prove his love to her before she would consider him a worthy suitor. The young man, Kitch-iti-kipi, asked what he had to do.

The woman responded, "You must go out on the waters of the spring in your canoe. I shall leap down from a tree on the water's edge and when I do, you must catch me."

It may have sounded crazy, but the chieftain was willing to try anything to win the love of this seductive woman. He launched his canoe onto the water and while drifting and waiting for his love, the canoe overturned, and he was killed.

While this tragedy played out, the woman was in the Native American village with her friends laughing at the stupidity of the young chieftain. The big springs was named in Kitch-iti-kipi's memory.

Native American legends usually teach a moral point. It's hard to find it in this story. You may prefer the story associated with Bellaire's generosity as the takeaway from Kitch-iti-kipi history.

Other stories are told about the spring. It is alleged that if you place a drop of honey on a piece of birch bark dipped into Kitch-iti-kipi and present it to a loved one, you will win their affection forever.

Yet another legend promises that if you take a small piece of tamarack bark from a tree growing on the banks of Kitch-iti-kipi, grind that bark with mortar and pestle, and place it in an individual's empty pocket, it will be replaced by glittering gold at exactly midnight.

• Book with a Tie to Kitch-iti-kipi

Carole Lynn Hare, ***The Legend of Kitch-iti-kipi*** (40-pages with some black and white illustrations). The author notes that many of the legends surrounding Kitch-iti-kipi are folk tales, some made up by John Bellaire to entice people to the Big Spring. Hare says her book tells the authentic legend of Kitch-iti-kipi passed down orally in her Native American family for more than 100 years. When Hare's great grandaunt died, she left the story written in a notebook. That notebook became Hare's inspiration for *The Legend of Kitch-iti-kipi.*

29. Manistique

Manistique, population 2,084 in 2020, invites you to "Come play with us, come stay with us." Like so many places in the U.P., Manistique is a warm and friendly and charming waterfront community. Located on the north shore of Lake Michigan at the mouth of the Manistique River, the city welcomes all seasons including winter.

In 1860 Charles Harvey established a community at Manistique and called it Epsport to honor his wife's family name. The name was later changed to Monistique to match the river's name. Monistique is derived from *Onamanitikong*, a Native American word meaning vermilion which described the reddish color of the river's water. When the village name was registered with the state, an "a" erroneously replaced the "o" and Monistique became Manistique. In 1901 the village grew to a city. It nicknamed itself "The Emerald City," not for the *Wizard of Oz*, but more likely for the emerald-colored waters of Kitch-iti-kipi spring (See Kitchi-iti-kipi in the guide.)

• Museums

Lake Effect Arts, 212 South Cedar at the corner of Oak, near the lighthouse and downtown. This nonprofit organization depends primarily on donations and grants to encourage participation in the arts in Schoolcraft County. You will find affordable art by local artists, and a helpful and welcoming staff.

<<>>

Manistique Water Tower, River Road, is a beautifully restored, Roman-style, brick water tower built in 1922. The octagonal tower stands 200 feet tall and has a 200,000-gallon capacity. The grounds include a farmhouse and other buildings you can tour. The small park-museum is supported by the Manistique County Historical Society.

• Beaches, Parks, and Trails

Indian Lake State Park, 8970 West County Road 442, is located on Indian Lake, and is six miles long and three miles wide, making it the fourth largest inland lake in the Upper Peninsula. The park provides picnic tables, grills, a shallow swimming beach, hunting, fishing, canoeing, kayaking, hiking, snowmobiling, cross-country skiing, and beautiful relaxing views of the serene lake. This is mostly an RV park, and it is often crowded. You will need a state park pass for admission.

<<>>

The Manistique Boardwalk and River Walk, extends 1.83 miles from the eastern city limits, under the US 2 Bridge, and into the downtown district. The boardwalk was first constructed in 1991. Expansion and improvements continue. There are picnic grounds, wildflowers, interpretive signs, and wildlife along the way. The Boardwalk has a fishing pier. You can access the Lighthouse from the cement pier, but the City of Manistique doesn't own the picturesque red lighthouse. You walk to the privately owned light at your own risk, especially if it's a windy day.

<<>>

Palm Book State Park. (See Kitch-iti-kipi in this guide.)

• Another Stop to Consider

Thompson State Fish Hatchery, 944 South State Highway M-149, opened in 1922. The hatchery produces Chinook salmon, steelhead, and walleye for both inland and Great Lakes waters. The hatchery is open to the public for self-guided educational tours if you have an interest in seeing how a fish hatchery operates.

• LIGHTHOUSE

The Manistique East Breakwater Light, in the Manistique Harbor, is a square-plan tower about 38 feet tall on a cast concrete foundation. The tower was constructed of steel plates bolted together and attached to the foundation. The light was first lit in 1916, automated in 1969, auctioned and bought by a private individual in 2013. The light is listed on the National Register of Historical Places.

The Manistique East Breakwater Light.
Courtesy of Bob Royce.

• SHIPWRECK

A strong storm struck the northern shoreline of Lake Michigan near Manistique on April 19, 2020. The winds whipped the sand into a frenzy. In the aftermath, a local man walked the beach near his home and came upon the bones of an old ship.

Not even a coronavirus quarantine stopped the curious beachcomber and the Michigan Shipwreck Research Association, which he contacted, from unraveling the mystery ship's identity.

Normally the MSRA would have gone to the wreck site and carried out an extensive investigation, but stay-at-home orders prevented travel. The MSRA knew the fickle sands could easily rebury the ship, and they were eager to learn its identity before that happened. The beachcomber took pictures and detailed measurements, and through his joint efforts with the MSRA, the ship was identified within the day as the ***R. Kanters***, a two-masted schooner named after its owner, Rokus Kanters, who was the mayor of Holland from 1885 to 1886.

The *R. Kanters* hauled various cargos through the Great Lakes in the late 1800s. Its home ports were Holland and Grand Haven. On September 7, 1903, the *R. Kanters* departed Manistique, but before crossing from the bay into open lake, the schooner was blown ashore and stranded near where the mystery ship was discovered. It is believed that over time the *R. Kanters* broke into pieces leaving debris buried in the sand.

• Books with Ties to Manistique

Dennis Cuesta, ***Stuck in Manistique***. Cuesta, a native of California, attended the University of Michigan and remained in the Upper Midwest during his early career. *Stuck in Manistique* is Cuesta's first novel. The idea came from an experience early in his marriage when he and his wife got stuck in Manistique. The story tells of a young man who had never heard of the small town before the death of his estranged aunt who left him, among other things, a B&B in Manistique. Settling his aunt's affairs thrusts the hero headlong into a situation filled with secrets and promise.

<<>>

Jen Hager, ***Miles from Manistique***. Peter should be worried when he and his friend Jeremy are involved in an accident that leaves them snowbound and isolated with no cell phone reception in Michigan's Upper Peninsula near Manistique. Worry isn't exactly Peter's prime emotion when he stumbles to a remote cabin, and his knock on the door is answered by two beautiful cousins. Maybe Peter's stroke of good fortune isn't such good luck after all. The young women have secrets, clues to which are written in a diary inside a trunk in the attic.

<<>>

M. Vonciel LeDuc and Schoolcraft County Historical Society, ***Manistique***. Natural resources turned many towns in the Upper Peninsula into boomtowns. This is Manistique's history from the Native Americans and occasional fur trader and missionary, through the lumber era to today's tourism.

30. GULLIVER

Gulliver is an unincorporated community with a 2010 population of 624. It draws visitors to the pristine beaches of its four inland lakes: Gulliver Lake, McDonald Lake, Clear Lake, and Little Muddy Lake, as well as to the shore of northern Lake Michigan. During the mid-1800s, Seul Choix Point was the center of a thriving fishing community, but today, only the lighthouse complex remains active. The Seul Choix Point Lighthouse is an operational light and the only working light on the northern shores of Lake Michigan.

• LIGHTHOUSE

Seul Choix Point Lighthouse, 3183 County Road 431. Pronounced locally as SIS-shwa but in true French as SEL-Shwa. The English translation of the name means Last

Choice, but it was the only choice for a safe harbor when storms blew across Lake Michigan.

The lighthouse has been in operation since 1895 and is currently automated. Along with the grounds, it is a museum operated by volunteers of the Gulliver Historical Society in cooperation with the Department of Natural Resources.

The two-story, red-brick attached keepers house accommodated two families. Several rooms were added to the original structure. The living quarters have been restored and decorated in period furniture from the early 1900s. Visitors can climb the lighthouse tower.

The lighthouse grounds have the original outbuildings including an explosives storehouse and the fog signal building. An old wood fish net dryer has been moved to the lawn near the house. The fog signal building has been repurposed as a gift shop. The Seul Choix Point Lighthouse is a Michigan Historic Site and a National Historic Landmark.

• Books With Ties to Seul Choix Point Lighthouse

Several books have been written about haunted lighthouses. A handful specifically focus on Seul Choix. The Museum Gift Shop carries an interesting selection.

• Ghost Story

Ghost of Seul Choix Lighthouse. Joseph Willie Townsend was the keeper of the lighthouse from 1902 to 1910 when he died in an upstairs bedroom. His death was attributed to consumption, but the diagnosis may not have been precise. Other accounts suggest he succumbed to lung cancer related to his lifelong habit of smoking cigars.

Townsend's body was prepared for burial. He lay in state in the parlor until his relatives could travel from distances to pay their respects. After his wake, the body was stored in the basement because the frozen ground couldn't be dug until spring.

What series of events keep Mr. Townsend's spirit in the century-old lighthouse is uncertain, but many sources and reports swear his ghost refuses to abandon its beloved lighthouse.

Townsend's wife forbade him to bring his stinking cigars in the house. Today, cigar smoke is often smelled in the house. Maybe Townsend likes the freedom he now has to ignore his wife's mandate.

Even stranger is current evidence that Townsend continues to express his displeasure with the American way of setting a table. After his death, parts from a kitchen table were found in the basement and taken upstairs and reassembled. More than 100 times, the place settings and the chairs have been disturbed. Forks are turned upside down, placed on the edge of a plate, or formed into a cross with a knife.

There is also the story of a salesman who came to the premises to offer an estimate for installing an alarm system. The man walked through the lighthouse, taking notes as he went. When he left the house, he locked the door behind him and returned to his car where he sat working on the cost proposal he intended to present. He looked back toward the house for a moment and saw Joseph Townsend staring at him from one of the windows. He was so rattled that he started the car, drove away, and let someone else have the job.

Other visitors to the lighthouse have reported seeing Townsend looking at them from a wall mirror.

Don't let the haunting deter you. Joseph Townsend is a friendly ghost who wants you to enjoy his lighthouse as much as he did.

Seul Choix Lighthouse. Courtesy of Pixabay Free Images.

The journey around Michigan's Coastal Waterways will now take you back to St. Ignace where you'll cross back over the Mackinac Bridge and begin your exploration of the Sunset Coasts. Book Three, *Exploring Michigan's Sunset Coasts* starts with Cross Village. Mackinaw City is included in Book One, *Exploring Michigan's Sunrise Coasts.*

Appendix One—Five favorite recipes from the U.P.

Since travel books cannot keep up with restaurant openings and closings, this guide offers instead a sampling of recipes with Yooper connections, starting with Whitefish.

Mackinac *Island and the Upper Peninsula are famous for whitefish. Michigan is also the place to catch walleye, perch, salmon, and trout.*

Beer Battered Whitefish

Ingredients

½ cup cornstarch
1½ tsp baking powder
¾ tsp salt
½ tsp Creole seasoning*
¼ tsp paprika
¼ tsp cayenne pepper
1 cup all-purpose flour, divided
½ cup 2% milk
1/3 cup beer
2 cups finely crushed unsalted saltine crackers (about 40)
1½ pounds fresh or frozen whitefish
oil for deep-fat frying

Directions

1. In a shallow bowl, combine the cornstarch, baking powder, salt, Creole seasoning, paprika, cayenne, and ½ cup flour. Stir in milk and beer until batter is smooth. Place finely crushed crackers and remaining flour in separate shallow bowls. Coat filets with flour, dip in batter, and then coat with crackers.
2. In an electric skillet or deep-fat fryer, heat oil to 375 degrees. Fry fish in batches for 2-3 minutes on each side or until golden brown. Drain on paper towels. Yield: 4 servings.

Notes

*The following spices may be substituted for ½ tsp Creole seasoning: ¼ tsp ground cumin, and cayenne pepper to taste.

You can substitute walleye or perch filets in this recipe.

There probably is no recipe with stronger ties to Michigan's Upper Peninsula than Pasties [pronounced pass tees]. These sealed pies were made as a portable lunch for miners in the upper peninsula. They have continued to be popular long after mining ceased to be the economic mainstay.

Cornish Finnish Michigan Pasties

Ingredients

4½ cups all-purpose flour
1 cup shortening
1¼ cups ice water
1 tsp salt
5½ cups thinly sliced potatoes
2 carrots, shredded
1 onion
½ cup diced rutabaga
1½ pounds lean ground beef
½ pound lean ground pork
1 Tbsp salt
1 tsp ground black pepper
1½ tsp monosodium glutamate (MSG)
1 cube beef bouillon
½ cup hot water

Directions

1. Whisk together flour and salt in a large bowl. Cut in shortening. Make a well in the center of the mixture and quickly stir in ice water. Form dough into a ball. Set aside.
2. Dissolve the bouillon cube in the hot water. Combine uncooked vegetables, uncooked meats, salt, pepper, monosodium glutamate, and bouillon.
3. Roll out pastry dough into 6 x 8-inch rectangles. Place about 1½ cups of filling in the center of each rectangle. Bring 6-inch sides together and seal. Cut a slit in the top of each pasty. Place on baking pans (preferably not shiny or Teflon coated).
4. Bake at 425 degrees for 45 minutes.

Delicious crepe-like pancakes served with warmed maple syrup, fruit, or a sprinkle of confectioners' sugar.

Finnish Pancakes

Ingredients

1 cup milk
2 Tbsp butter, melted
2 eggs
½ cup all-purpose flour
1 tsp baking powder
½ tsp vanilla extract
zest of ½ lemon
½ tsp salt

Directions

1. Pour milk into a microwave-safe bowl. Heat in the microwave until slightly warm, 20 to 30 seconds. Whisk in melted butter. Whisk in eggs. Add flour, baking powder, vanilla extract, lemon zest, and salt. Whisk or mix on low beater setting to make a smooth batter.

2. Heat a lightly oiled griddle over medium-high heat. Drop batter by large spoonsful onto the griddle and cook until bottom is golden brown, 2 to 3 minutes. Flip and cook until browned on the other side, 2 to 3 minutes. Repeat with remaining batter. Recipe makes 10 pancakes but can be doubled or tripled.

Finnish Pancakes.
Courtesy of Pixabay Free Images.

This soup is served in some Michigan Upper Peninsula restaurants.

Kielbasa and Sauerkraut Soup

Ingredients

4 oz bacon, cooked and diced (optional)
1 pound Polish kielbasa, sliced (optional)
½ cup cooked, diced chicken (optional)
1 onion, diced
2 carrots, thinly diced
2 sticks celery, thinly diced
3 cloves garlic, chopped
8 ounces sliced mushrooms
1 tsp smoked hot paprika
4 cups chicken or vegetable broth
2 cups sauerkraut, drained
2 potatoes, diced
½ cup quinoa (optional)
1 (15 ounce) can white beans, drained and rinsed
salt and pepper to taste

Directions

1. Cook bacon in a large sauce pot over medium high heat until crisp. Set aside. Add sausage to the bacon grease and cook until browned on both sides. Set aside.
2. Add the onion, carrots, and celery to the pan and cook until tender, about 5-7 minutes. Add garlic, mushrooms, and paprika and cook until fragrant, about a minute.
3. Add broth, sauerkraut, potatoes, quinoa, beans, bacon, sausage, and chicken. Bring to boil, reduce heat, and simmer until quinoa and potatoes are tender, about 15-20 minutes. Season with salt and pepper to taste.

Vegetarian Option: Omit bacon, sausage, and chicken. Use vegetable broth. Cook onions in 1 Tbsp vegetable oil.

Tip: Top with sour cream and/or grainy mustard and serve with rye bread.

As any Michigan Hunter knows, you need a good recipe for venison. This one simmers to tender perfection.

Slow Cooker Venison Roast

Ingredients

3 pounds boneless venison roast
1 large onion, sliced
1 Tbsp soy sauce
1 Tbsp Worcestershire sauce
1 Tbsp garlic salt
¼ tsp ground black pepper
1 (1 ounce) package dry onion soup mix
6 ounces sliced mushrooms (optional)
2 carrots, sliced in thin diagonals
1 tsp fresh chopped rosemary
2 large russet potatoes, peeled and cut into large chunks
1 (10.75 ounce) can condensed cream of mushroom soup
rosemary sprigs for garnish

Directions

1. Put cleaned meat in slow cooker and cover with onion, carrots, and mushrooms. Sprinkle with soy sauce, Worcestershire sauce, garlic salt, rosemary, and pepper.
2. In a small bowl, combine the soup mix and the soup. Mix together and pour over venison.
3. Cook on low setting for six hours.

Slow Cooker Venison Roast.
Courtesy of Pixabay Free Images.

Appendix Two—An Inland Trip to Iron Mountain

Iron Mountain is 78 miles south of Marquette or 53 miles east of Escanaba. The **Millie Mine Bat Cave**, Mine Shaft, Park Avenue off East A Street, is a tourist stop the likes of which you won't encounter anywhere else in Michigan. A million bats, give or take a few hundred, make an abandoned vertical iron mine their home. The bats are free to fly about at will, but a special grate prevents people from falling into the shaft while they observe the creatures. Best times to watch the activity is at dusk, and the best months are April to May and September to October when bats are entering or leaving the mine during hibernation. A self-guided interpretive program educates visitors about the benefits of bats. The mine is designated an official Michigan Wildlife Viewing Area.

Other things to see or do in Iron Mountain include **Pine Mountain**, the largest artificial ski jump in the U.S., with an outdoor recreation area of 18 trails for the alpine skier. Snowboarders appreciate the Terrain Park and Half Pipe.

Pine Mountain Ski Jump. Courtesy of Pixabay Free Images.

Also consider stops at the **WWII Glider and Military Museum**, the **Cornish Pumping Engine and Mining Museum**, and the **Fumee Lake Natural Area** with abundant scenery, varied terrain, and more than 11 miles of trails.

Index

Acknowledgements

My biggest debt of gratitude is owed to my husband. He worked doggedly to resolve my computer issues and helped me in a gazillion ways. He is even happier than I am to see this project completed.

Exploring Michigan's Upper Peninsula Coasts is part of a three-volume series that is my way of saying thanks to my home state for providing a safe, nurturing, and beautiful place to grow up. What started as a little guide with an anticipated three hundred pages turned into a whopping 900+ pages and three books. That's love.

Working on these travel books gave me a special awe for the generosity of strangers. Tim Trombley gave me permission to use his gorgeous photograph of Spray Falls on the front cover of *Exploring Michigan's Upper Peninsula Coasts*. To see more of Tim's photography, check his website at www.greatlakesphotography.net.

Gary Martin permitted me to use his incomparable lighthouse photos. Over the months, he checked thousands of files and made any changes I requested. His patience was never ending. Visit www.coastalbeacons.com to see more examples of his amazing work.

For their many kindnesses, I thank the business owners, museum staff, chambers of commerce, historical societies, librarians, and Upper Peninsula residents who shared their time and stories.

In no particular order, I am indebted to Jennifer Granholm, Jessie Voigts, Kathi Hyatt, Julaina Kleist-Corwin, Susan and Joe Jurkiewicz, Linda Cutler, Vee Byrum, Paula Chinick, Neva Hodges, Lani Longshore, Julie Rosas, Mimi Wirtanen, Diane Herron, Jordan Bernal, Maureen Scully, George Cramer, Margie Lampel, Nancy Peck, and especially Violet Moore. She is the Chicago Manual of Style expert extraordinaire. She is also a walking encyclopedia of useful information for any writing endeavor. Without the patience and creative assistance of Nina Rosas, these books would remain coverless.

To everyone above, and the many I may have overlooked, thank you one and all.

About the Author

Julie Albrecht Royce was born in Lexington and raised in the small town of Sandusky in Michigan's Thumb. After retiring as a Michigan First Assistant Attorney General, she turned to her love of writing and authored two travel books: *Traveling Michigan's Thumb* and *Traveling Michigan's Sunset* Coast.

She has authored two novels, *PILZ,* a crime thriller, and *Ardent Spirit,* the fictionalized biography of Magdelaine LaFramboise, an Odawa-French fur trader born in the Michigan Territory in 1780.

Ms. Royce has written magazine articles, has been included in several anthologies, and has had stories accepted in the *California Writers Club Literary Review.* In her three-book travel series (*Exploring Michigan's Sunrise Coasts, Exploring Michigan's Upper Peninsula Coasts*, and *Exploring Michigan's Sunset Coasts*), she comes full circle back to her love of Michigan and the Great Lakes.

www.ingramcontent.com/pod-product-compliance
Ingram Content Group UK Ltd.
Pitfield, Milton Keynes, MK11 3LW, UK
UKHW022025190726
13853UKWH00005B/2116

9 798985 503715